DATE DUE

In-Service Education
for Teachers

In-Service Education

for Teachers

JOHN CLIFTON MOFFITT

Superintendent, Provo City Schools
Provo, Utah

1963
The Center for Applied Research in Education, Inc.
Washington, D.C.

Foreword

This book is addressed to all those in the teaching profession who feel the need for professional growth in our rapidly changing world. The main thesis of the author, Dr. John Clifton Moffitt, is in the statement "that injustices to children and youth will be certain unless education for teachers increases in quality and quantity, after teaching commences."

Although the author maintains that the teaching profession should require vigorous preservice education, his main emphasis is on in-service education programs for all professionals. This, he contends, should be done through better use of the findings of research and through research as a means of professional growth while in service.

How shall in-service education be organized? What is the role of the individual teacher in relation to the group? How are the results of in-service education programs evaluated? These are but a few of the problems explored in this challenging volume.

One of the unique contributions of this book is the description of the plan of the six-year "merit" study developed in Dr. Moffitt's own school system at Provo, Utah. The major problem in the Provo study was to find an objective way to "define" or "describe" the qualitative aspects of teaching. An examination of the Provo study lends support to conclusions made in this volume.

This challenging monograph by Dr. Moffitt will add much to the better professional literature of our day.

MARION G. MERKLEY
State Superintendent of Public Instruction
Salt Lake City, Utah

v

Contents

CONTENTS

CHAPTER VI

In-Service Education Through Democratic Processes

CHAPTER VII

In-Service Education and Professional Relations

In-Service Education
for Teachers

CHAPTER I

The Need for Continuous
Education of Teachers

Education of Teachers in a Changing Society

The quality of education in the United States reflects the needs and aspirations of the people. These needs and aspirations during the last half of the twentieth century are as different from those of earlier years as the society today is different from that of earlier centuries. Change came slowly during the first two hundred years of our history, in spite of the fact that within that time a new nation of people had arisen. As the slowly expanding frontier tended to attract more people westward, there came a noticeable breakdown of the church controls and church-directed education that had prevailed in earlier years.

Separated from older nations by the span of oceans, difficult transportation, and slow communication, it was nearly impossible to find teachers educationally prepared to meet the needs of this young country. Consequently, many of the teachers were not well educated and gave little thought to improving their skills while they were teaching. It is claimed by some that many teachers of that time were incapable of adequate adjustment to the normal demands of society and consequently "turned" to teaching. Some of these teachers were former criminals; others were generally incompetent and immature.[1]

The quality of teachers near the midpoint of the last century may be noted in a series of annual reports by Horace Mann. Mann recognized the incompetency of large numbers of those who were teaching. In 1842 he declared that many were teaching whose "services were not merely valueless but pernicious" and who were retained as teachers because the law failed to delegate to a specific

---

[1] Anthony C. LaBue, "Teacher Certification in the United States: A Brief History," *The Journal of Teacher Education*, Vol. XI, No. 2 (June, 1960), 147–72.

agency the legal power to dismiss them. In his *Sixth Annual Report* he declared that five years earlier "between three and four hundred of our public schools were annually brought to a violent termination" because of "rebellious scholars" or "gross incompetency on the part of teachers." [2]

In his 1844 report Mann stated that it appeared from the school committee reports "that in the school year 1842–43 twenty-six schools were broken up through the incompetency of teachers." [3]

In 1844 Massachusetts enacted a law giving the school committee the legal right to dismiss teachers for incompetency, and "subsequent to the enactment of the law, the number [of schools] discontinued, or suspended, for the same cause [incompetency] was sixty-five—an increase of fifty per cent." [4]

The historians of education in the United States typically declare that a substantial number of those earlier teachers were itinerant wanderers, odd in both dress and behavior, frequently intemperate, and brutally severe in their discipline of students. [5]

Changes in the quality of teachers as a result of teacher education came tardily. The first state normal school was opened at Lexington, Massachusetts, in the late 1830's. These were small institutions and grew slowly, but they did establish the foundation upon which teacher education institutions were built later.

New social and economic forces arising in the early years of this century were such that demands were made for education beyond the elementary schools. The curriculum of the normal school, established for elementary teachers, did not meet the needs of high school teachers. Under these circumstances the normal schools began the transition to teachers colleges.

Teacher Training Institutions in Transition

Teachers colleges had their growth during the earlier decades of this century. This growth tended to parallel the growth of high

---

2 Horace Mann, *Sixth Annual Report,* facsimile ed. (Boston: Dutton and Wentworth, 1843), p. 38.

3 Horace Mann, *Eighth Annual Report,* facsimile ed. (Boston: Dutton and Wentworth, 1845), p. 66.

4 Horace Mann, *Ninth Annual Report,* facsimile ed. (Boston: Dutton and Wentworth, 1846), p. 39.

5 Ellwood P. Cubberly, *Public Education in the United States* (Boston: Houghton Mifflin Company, 1947), p. 54.

schools. Gradually, normal schools either ceased to exist or were converted into teachers colleges. Like the normal school, the teachers college became a significant institution for educating teachers for American schools. Like its predecessor, however, the teachers college—its staff and curriculum—eventually became inadequate. The attempt to adapt to the changing needs of the times brought about a transition to state colleges and state universities. From 1910 to the middle of the century, plans and programs for educating teachers changed greatly. Increased understanding of children and numerous societal changes—both national and international—with the problems inherent therein presented new demands for teacher competency.

The college or department of education commonly existing at present is becoming one of several colleges or departments. These are institutions of status and are becoming comparable to other graduate and professional schools. One writer states that the teachers college will have been only "a temporary phenomenon in American higher education." [6]

Increasing Demands for Teacher Education

The growing insistence for more effective teaching has paralleled the increasing complexity of our changing society. Some demands have grown gradually; others have come suddenly and follow closely the challenging national and international developments of our time.

Our accumulation of knowledge during recent years has been rapid. Research, scientific experimentation, and new explorations have revealed facts heretofore unknown. The race between education and catastrophe was never so closely run. It now appears certain that injustices to children and youth will be inevitable unless education for teachers increases in quality and quantity, both before and after teaching commences.

This increasing need for in-service learning on the part of teachers does not alter an increasing need for more education preparatory to teaching. Although leaders in the teaching profession for

---

[6] Karl W. Bigelow, "The Passing of the Teachers College," *Teachers College Record*, Vol. 58, No. 8 (1957), 411.

more than a decade have advocated a bachelor's degree as a minimum for all teachers, now many maintain that an additional year is essential [7] and some suggest that in addition to this year of clinical experience with a master teacher is or should be a prerequisite to successful teaching.

Lambert has predicted that "within the next decade or so, the bachelor's degree is going to be outmoded. . . ." He further states: "Already, almost half of the nation's high school teachers possess a master's degree." [8]

Many teachers in the nation's elementary schools, for example, did not receive adequate science education as undergraduate students. The great upsurge of demands for early science education requires that teachers become better informed of (a) added subject matter, (b) improved methods of teaching in the areas of science, and (c) new attitudes and skills in the use of scientific procedures transferred to other fields of learning.[9]

The mature teacher and the beginning teacher, the good and not-so-good, all need to extend their knowledge and change their patterns of teaching as research may direct. Spears has said: "The teacher who experiences a top salary schedule is just as deserving and as needful of supervisory leadership as the teacher in a system that has a low salary scale." [10]

The teaching profession is not unique in this respect: other professions are requiring added preservice and in-service education as more and more research alters practices. As knowledge about human growth and other specialized areas is increased, a parallel need exists for more specialists in the schools.

Not only is more now known in subject matter areas, but curriculum adjustments are many and constant. Considerable evidence exists that some subjects may be taught with good results in earlier grades than has been the custom formerly. Mature teachers who

---

[7] Sam M. Lambert, "Investing in Quality Education," *Phi Delta Kappan,* Vol. 43, No. 3 (December), 115.

[8] Sam M. Lambert, "Educational Growth and Change Lie Ahead in the 1960's," *National Education Association Journal,* Vol. 49, No. 9 (December, 1960), 46.

[9] Robert Karplus, "The Science Curriculum—One Approach," *Elementary School Journal,* Vol. 62, No. 5 (February, 1962), 243.

[10] Harold Spears, *Curriculum Planning Through In-Service Programs* (Englewood Cliffs, N.J.: Prentice-Hall, Inc., 1957), p. 29.

have not learned how much and under what circumstances team teaching may be most effective, or who know little or nothing about the use of a wide array of teaching machines, or who do not know the circumstances under which programmed learning pays educational dividends, are on an educational island and remote from modern school innovations.

The Teaching Profession and Certification Requirements

The teaching profession, through its own associations, has done much since World War II to increase the education of the nation's teachers. Certification requirements have been raised substantially as a result of state and national association demands presented to certifying agencies. In spite of teacher shortages and enlarged enrollments, the associations have insisted on better prepared teachers.

The conspicuous increase of education of elementary teachers may be noted by a statement in the April, 1959, *NEA Research Bulletin*:

> Without question, the greatest postwar achievement in American education has been a dramatic upgrading of the entire corps of elementary-school teachers. The typical teacher today has more than one full year of college preparation beyond that of the typical teacher 10 years ago. This has been achieved despite the impact of an enrollment increase of 17,341,000 to 24,341,000.[11]

In-Service Training Needs for Beginning Teachers

As indicated above, increased birth rates, expansion of school programs, and replacement of uncertified teachers all create teacher shortages which in turn require large numbers of people to enter the teaching profession each school year.[12] Under such circumstances school systems must have effective in-service teacher education programs.

The magnitude of the challenge for in-service education of new teachers may be noted by a statement in a 1959 *NEA Research Bulletin* which claims that "over the past 10 years the instructional

---

11 *NEA Research Bulletin*, Vol. XXXVII, No. 2 (April, 1959), 58.
12 *NEA Research Bulletin*, Vol. XXXIX, No. 1 (February, 1961), 28.

staff has increased 50.3 per cent to a total of 1,395,940 for the school year 1958–59." [13]

Regardless of the quantity and quality of academic education received in a college or university, a teacher new to any given school system needs in-service education. Specific assignments cannot be foreseen by institutions that provide the preservice education.

The beginning teacher enters into a strange and completely new situation. For many, it is the first real job the teacher has had, with the responsibilities attached thereto. Everything is strange. Commonly, he is unacquainted with the other teachers, the principal, or the administrative or supervisory personnel. The students are strange, and often the community is one about which he has little knowledge.

To combat this feeling of strangeness and the frequent reluctance to ask the right questions of the right people, some writers have proposed that beginning teacher associations be established.[14] The primary purpose of such associations would be to encourage teachers with limited knowhow to exchange experiences and ask and answer questions without concern or fear of criticism from those who have had years of teaching service.

Teaching is learning, and much of it tends to be repeated until it becomes a habit. Teaching performance of poor quality may be learned as readily as if it were good. In fact, the chances are that it will be learned more quickly. It appears to be easier to be authoritarian, defensive, and repetitive than it is to be democratic, sharing, and versatile. An all too common error is the assumption that teaching is of excellent quality when the teacher has good "control" and order prevails.

Numerous school systems throughout the country classify beginning teachers as probationary teachers. Frequently, teachers remain on probation for two or three years. This appears to be in recognition of the fact that these are years in which young teachers need special in-service education. Commonly, the colleges from which teachers graduate request evaluations of their former students during the first year or two of teaching. Occasionally, the college provides some assistance to the beginning teacher. Such a college

---

[13] *NEA Research Bulletin*, Vol. XXXVII, No. 1 (February, 1959), 3.

[14] R. A. C. Oliver, *The Training of Teachers in Universities* (London: University of London Press, Ltd., 1943), p. 42.

training program can be most effective if it is coordinated with the in-service training of the school system.

The amount and the need for assistance as expressed by beginning teachers is apparent from a survey of urban communities made by the Research Department of the National Education Association. One-third of all such teachers reporting in 1954–55 said they received "some" help from principals. More than 30 per cent declared they received little or no help, and 36.2 per cent stated they received much help. The greatest amount of help provided to first-year teachers came from fellow teachers.[15]

Criticisms of Education

A series of incidents have occurred since the close of World War II that have caused certain segments of the public to demand teaching of a better quality. From the war we learned (as we had learned before from World War I) that the strength of a nation is largely dependent upon the kind and amount of education of its people.

With or without sufficient evidence to justify their actions, some citizens have developed strong convictions that the schools of the United States are not adequately teaching children and youth to cope with the problems they are inheriting. The teachers and the colleges that prepare and teach the teachers are given the blame for this alleged weakness.

Teacher education is responding to constructive criticism. Changes are already in process. The entire program is under study and, as experimentation with new programs proves fruitful, more changes will be made. Obviously, the many institutions that educate teachers cannot all be alike for each is essentially free to choose its own course. It is probably this situation which caused Lieberman to say: "Teacher education in the United States is in a state of chaos." [16]

Proper education of the nation's teachers is and should be the concern of every citizen. It is the education of teachers that deter-

---

15 "First-Year Teachers in 1954–55," *NEA Research Bulletin,* Vol. XXIV, No. 1 (February, 1956), 33.

16 Myron Lieberman, "Teacher Education and the Secondary Curriculum— U. S. A.," *The Secondary School Curriculum: The Yearbook of Education, 1958* (New York: Harcourt, Brace & World, Inc., 1958), p. 318.

mines the quality of learning and therefore the quality of the people of this country. Now and in years to come teachers must become sensitive to new and challenging responsibilities. The increase of knowledge is as profound as it is inspiring. This accumulation of knowledge appears to be endless and will be accelerated as the years go by. Teachers of our time and those in the future must accept this unparalleled opportunity for professional growth as they teach. To do otherwise would be to threaten the expanding ideals of this democracy. The sensitivity of teachers to the array of problems with which they are confronted may be noted by their eagerness for continuous growth. It therefore appears safe to conclude that the quality of any school system may largely be determined by the quality of the in-service educational programs involving the total professional staff.

CHAPTER II

The Impact of Change

The Force of Technology

This is an age of change. It requires new and rapid adjustments. Its impact on education is an ongoing challenge. It is the basic reason determining the need for continuous education of all people and particularly of all teachers. Without continuing study, teacher knowledge and teacher performance soon become obsolete. No one is ever completely educated—at most one can only be a student of the daily incidents as they occur. The important changes are too many to list. However, some are selected to indicate the need for in-service education of teachers.

One example of change is in the role of government. No agency concerned with people has made a more extensive change during this century than has government. Not only has its magnitude and complexity grown, but the new issues and problems with which it is confronted each hour of the day must have some understanding by American people. Within the lifetime of parents of children now in school, the United States has expanded and extended from a young and inconspicuous republic to a world power. Its interests, both political and material, are all over this world and now extending to other planets. Our "concerns" and our "interests" are much more national and international in scope than was the case in the lives of former generations. Local interests and problems are relatively much less important, and in their place have come national and international issues of greater magnitude.

The role of education in producing and directing change at this hour of history is a major responsibility. The competition for power among nations indicates the United States cannot remain the great force that it is unless it does change. This is in part due to the fact that again some older countries are becoming relatively stronger, and new countries that had made little or no change for centuries are becoming modern powers.

9

Changes Have Added to Our Store of Knowledge

The speed with which we travel and the ease with which we communicate make new understandings of people everywhere a necessity. Worldwide television and other mass media greatly add to the number of new facts and new situations that must be understood. The Chancellor of the University of Kansas has appropriately said: "The central fact of our age is the explosion of human knowledge. . . . We must realize that we are not dealing with mere change but with totally new dimensions." [1]

Much of the change that affects the schools is the result of pure and applied science. Increasingly, we are dependent upon the researcher and the highly educated not only to raise our standard of living but also to strengthen our economy and perpetuate our national welfare. Our dependence upon scientific skill in turn is dependent upon the quality of the education of those who are to become scientists.

A New Emphasis on Science Teaching

The upsurge of concern about the teaching of science has produced new methods and new content at all school levels. Karplus appropriately suggests that elementary school children can bridge the span from direct experiencing to abstract relationships and implications.[2]

The teaching of science has changed greatly during the past decade. The enactment by Congress of the National Defense Education Act has made it possible for many school systems to expand their science programs. Alterations and expansions of science laboratories is not uncommon, and a vast array of new equipment has been installed in schools at all levels.

Commonly, colleges and universities, individually or in cooperation with such agencies as the National Science Foundation, have sponsored workshops, institutes, and other intensive training courses

[1] Franklin D. Murphy, "Educational Dimensions for a Revolutionary Epoch," in *The Education of Teachers, Curriculum Programs, Report of the Kansas TEPS Conference* (Washington, D.C.: National Commission on Teacher Education and Professional Standards, National Education Association, 1959), p. 48.

[2] Robert Karplus, "The Science Curriculum—One Approach," *Elementary School Journal,* Vol. 62, No. 5 (February, 1962), 243–52.

intended to improve the quality of teaching below the college level. These media as sources of in-service education have become common during recent years.

The schools necessarily reflect the interests and needs of the society in which they exist. As John H. Fisher has said: "Whatever affects society affects the shcools." [3]

Many think of science as a product, but teachers must think of science as a process. They must regard it as a conceptual approach to the discovery of truth. The "product" of science is changing, but the attitude of science is permanent. With good teaching, it must become a part of each educated individual.

Mathematics as an Example of Curriculum Change

The schools have been accused of permitting a lag in the kind of teaching that is commonly done compared to that which should be done. This lag has two aspects. The subject matter, it is claimed, tends to be textbookish, stale, and antiquated, and the methods of teaching are too often the same as were used by teachers of an earlier generation. An important area of curriculum change may be noted in the case of mathematics and the newer methods of teaching it.

Speaking of newer mathematics, Price has said: "The twentieth century has been the golden age of mathematics, since more mathematics, and more profound mathematics, has been created in this period than during all the rest of history." [4]

World War II had a pronounced effect upon the curriculum, giving use to a new zest for mathematics and sicence. [5]

The upsurge of interest on the part of mathematics teachers may be noted by the fact that more than 2500 persons were in attendance at the thirty-eighth annual meeting of the National Council of Teachers of Mathematics (April 20–23, 1960). Interest was fo-

---

[3] John H. Fisher, "Steps into the Future," *The School Executive*, Vol. 75, No. 11 (July, 1956), 52–55.

[4] G. Baley Price, "Progress in Mathematics and Its Implications for the Schools," *The Revolution in School Mathematics* (Washington, D.C.: The National Council of Teachers of Mathematics), p. 1.

[5] *NEA Research Bulletin*, "The Nation's Schools After a Year of War," Vol. XXI, No. 2 (April, 1943), 41.

cused on both the new content and the new methods of teaching—
particularly machine teaching.[6]

The avowed purpose of this movement (that of re-examining
and modifying the teaching of mathematics) is to bring the teaching
of mathematics up to date by taking into account the changes that
have taken place in mathematics.[7]

Demands for Curriculum Revision

Changes in the world society are constant. New nations with new
governments and new values and purposes are coming into existence. In contrast to the revolutionary world of the present and the
curriculum changes that interpret it, the older curriculum was limited to the restricted and stable life of an earlier time. People then
had little knowledge or concern beyond the farm or the village
where they lived. Changes have been such that a high school student today learns more about what is happening in Russia or Burma
or any other part of the world than earlier students learned about
the village a few miles distant from their homes.

Change is the magic force that motivates continuous study and
alteration of the curriculum. Therefore, the teachers must be concerned not only with needed curriculum changes in the sciences and
mathematics but also with the total curriculum. It now is the teacher's serious business to know and to be able to interpret all important incidents in every part of the world. In spite of our speed and
power of production, texts and other books describing this political,
social, and economic world are too slow in reaching the students.
The teacher must be sensitive to the world in which he lives. If he
is to remain a major source of knowledge, he must keep abreast of
world events. With all that has been written and discussed about
continuous expansions and alterations of the curriculum, it must
be understood that the curriculum changes only as the teacher
changes it.

---

[6] M. H. Ahrent, "Newer Trends in Teaching Mathematics," *School and Society,*
Vol. 88, No. 2177 (September, 1960), 329–30.

[7] Daniel W. Snader, Conference Reporter of United States Office of Education,
The Leadership Role of State Supervisors of Mathematics, Bulletin No. 1 (Washington, D.C.: U.S. Office of Education, 1962), 11.

Better Understanding of Children
and Improved Teaching

It has been difficult to sever the past from the present in teaching methods. Many parents are concerned about teaching procedures that are "different" from those they remember.

Education has had its own experimental programs and has borrowed from other disciplines, particularly from the behavioral sciences. Much has been learned from child psychology about motivation, learning, and emotions.

From sociologists and social psychologists educators have learned much about the behavior of children and adults as they relate to others in a variety of situations. All these researches have had an influence in modifying educational procedures. Teachers of the first years of this century and earlier believed that an important ability of a successful teacher was that of "controlling" and "directing" students. Today's teachers have learned from experimental evidence that controlling is not an effective method of teaching. Basic concepts of democracy, a regard for students as important people, proper use of freedom, concern for satisfying human relations—all are important aspects of modern teaching. These are now well established after careful experimentation.

Most teachers engaged in modern in-service education programs maintain that the older traditional ways of teaching must be supplanted by what has been learned from careful research in education and in other disciplines. It is known, too, that the transition is difficult. Sharp points out that most teachers are trained in "traditional practices and values" and unless they are given extended help by others they will not change.[8]

Careful research studies have shown the uniqueness of the individual, the differences each one possesses. The making of curriculums which will meet the needs of all of the people while keeping individual differences paramount is a continuing and challenging problem. The Sixty-First Yearbook of the National Society for the Study of Education (1962, Part I) is devoted to "individualizing"

---

[8] George Sharp, *Curriculum Development As Re-education of the Teacher* (New York: Teachers College, Bureau of Publications, Columbia University, 1951), pp. 4–7.

instruction and emphasizes this responsibility of teachers. The authors recognize the fact that in a democracy we must have conformity in many matters but that at the same time our progress as a nation depends upon diversity.[9]

This same concept of diversity and conformity is noted in much of the educational literature. It is emphasized in Clarence H. Faust's *The High School in a New Era:*

> The teacher ought to be prepared to encourage uniqueness and difference rather than to require conformity. It is one of the most serious dangers of any highly organized society such as is ours, that it encourages, especially in times of stress, the development of the organization of man, the social and intellectual conformist, the well-balanced and well-adjusted individual, and tends to discourage, if not to suppress, the unique, the different, the independent, the pioneer.[10]

Cultural Cleavages and Intergroup Education

The greatest of all the problems this nation faces is international in scope. Within a generation, the United States has changed from a somewhat isolated position to one in which it has definite interests in and varied relations with every country on earth. As indicated above, improvements in transportation and communication have made all nations neighbors. Distance has no significance since the ratio of distance to time has changed so greatly. This change has brought all people closely together so suddenly that racial, cultural, and national differences cannot be resolved as readily as other changes are made. Centuries-old values that are deeply embedded in emotion obstruct intelligent understanding. Our values derive from such sources as Christianity, common law, or ethics of the western world; most of these are strange to the large majority of the world's population. Our new and easy contacts with foreign peoples are not readily producing the results we may desire. We

---

[9] Fred T. Tyler and William A. Brownell, "Facts and Issues: A Concluding Statement," in *Individualizing Instruction.* The Sixty-First Yearbook of the National Society for the Study of Education, Part I, Nelson B. Henry, ed. (Chicago: University of Chicago Press, 1962), pp. 316–27.

[10] Clarence H. Faust, "Essential Qualifications of Teachers for the New Era," in *The High School in a New Era,* Francis S. Chase and Harold A. Anderson, eds. (Washington, D.C.: National Education Association), pp. 124–25.

remain rich in material wealth; most of the others are poor. We live an average of three score and ten years with promise of increased longevity; their life expectancy is only half as long. We have changed our ways of living with great speed; they change slowly. We rely heavily upon education as the highway to a good and improving life; they often remain illiterate and superstitious. We look forward to the new; they rely on custom and tradition.

But "they" are not all the same, and "they" (in many subgroups) have diverse values. These are among forces that create and maintain the cleavages in our world. These differences persist and constitute a challenge to our concept of democracy.

Our new neighbors speak a language with which we are unfamiliar. They fear we would enslave or destroy them, and we in turn distrust them.

In this time of distrust, the schools are caught with definite challenges and suffer from uncertainty as to the course or courses that should be pursued. A large, powerful, and vocal segment of the public thinks, acts, and talks as if we are yet a nation in isolation, unaffected by and in no way related to other nations. Clifford P. Hooker maintains the schools must divest themselves of this attitude of isolationism, "remove the blindfolds from the youth of America," [11] and help children and youth understand their true role in understanding other nations.

Because teachers are inadequately solving these problems and keenly feel a need for in-service training that will help them toward solutions, some school systems now maintain workshops with the aid of anthropologists for the purpose of helping teachers to acquire a greater understanding on non-Western cultures.[12]

Innovations Suggest Changing Methods of Teaching

Within recent years, certainly since most of the present American teachers received their teacher education, many innovations (largely the result of applied science and technology) have emerged in some school systems. These include the use of films, tape recorders, tele-

---

[11] Clifford P. Hooker, "To Create An Enduring Society," *Phi Delta Kappan*, Vol. XLII, No. 9 (June, 1961), 374–78.

[12] Robert C. Hammock, "Cultural Orientation of American Teachers," *Educational Leadership*, Vol. 19, No. 8 (May, 1962), 497–500.

vision, and a variety of teaching machines, both for individual and group use. They also include an increasingly large number of programmed learning materials. Not only must the teacher learn how, when, and where to use these mechanical aids, but he must also learn the new philosophy of education of a given school system that adopts these aids to learning.

Such innovations as flexible scheduling, team teaching, and the use of programmed materials and teaching machines all tend to show the speed with which change occurs. Only those teachers who can carry on experimental or action research programs, analyze existing reports of research, and apply those concepts and techniques that are helpful in new and changing programs can enjoy the satisfaction that comes from diversified teaching.

Teachers Must Change

The attitude toward change differs from teacher to teacher as, in general, it does from person to person. Some things that are a challenge to one teacher are a threat to another. The more creative the ideas emerging from motivating challenges calling for radical departures from traditional ways of teaching, the greater will the threat appear to those who are made uncomfortable by change.

Many reasons and rationalizations may be found by teachers as they are faced with the challenge or opportunity to become a part of an in-service education program. Those who feel the least secure will likely be the first to erect the "protection of barriers." [13] around themselves.

It is not an easy accomplishment to bring about changes in ways of teaching in the curriculum. During the recent criticism of public education, some capable teachers and some excellent school systems have discarded progressive procedures and retreated to programs that were common and accepted years earlier.

The change ought not be too large or too sudden. Acceptance of the new will be more certain if minor concepts and insights are introduced gradually. The greater the satisfaction with traditional methods, the more difficult it will be to move the group toward new

---

[13] Earl C. Kelley and Marie I. Rasey, *Education and the Nature of Man* (New York: Harper & Row, Publishers, 1952), p. 79.

goals. In other words, if meaningful dissatisfactions with existing ways can parallel or precede anticipated changes, it will be easier to accept and adopt new behavior.

Mobility of Population

One change noticeable during this century is the increasing tendency for people to change their place of residence. Differing substantially from the time when the majority of families lived on farms, our technological age has forced rural people to find nonfarm employment. A large portion of these people "on the move" are young families with school-age children.

This trend has been accentuated since the beginning of World War II. People (frequently from cultural levels where unstable employment was already a problem) have migrated to industrial centers seeking new jobs. Millions of these are now centered in large cities, frequently creating serious social, economic, and educational problems. These are the disadvantaged [14] and are what Conant calls "social dynamite." [15]

Providing teachers who are prepared for the task of meeting the needs of these millions of disadvantaged children is a genuine challenge, both to the large city school systems and to the entire nation. Perhaps in no area is there greater need for in-service education of teachers than in these locations. The trend of mobility, however, is not directed exclusively toward the inside of large industrial cities. Twenty-five million people, or approximately 20 per cent of the population of the United States, are living today in houses other than those in which they lived one year ago. More young adults move than those of any other age group, but 27.8 per cent of all children aged one to four, inclusive, move each year.

Teachers themselves are among the mobile. They move from place to place, often to a community or section of a community with different cultural levels than they had formerly known. For example, Spears [16] points out that in San Francisco teachers are em-

[14] James Betchkal, "Rural Education: Caught in a Crossroads," *The Nation's Schools* (November, 1961), 84.

[15] James B. Conant, *Slums and Suburbs* (New York: McGraw-Hill Book Company, Inc.), pp. 1–147.

[16] Harold Spears, *Improving the Supervision of Instruction* (Englewood Cliffs, N.J.: Prentice-Hall, Inc., 1953), pp. 404–405.

ployed to occupy a "city position" and that thereafter they are assigned to a section of the city as needed. He states that these sections (a kind of a city within a city) differ significantly from one another. The ethnic and cultural backgrounds of these school communities differ widely in all of the large cities. All such situations require in-service education of teachers if they are to understand the people and the people's problems and needs as they relate to education.

The problem of transient children adjusting to a new environment is a challenge to teachers as well as to children. New and strange people and different and often unrelated curriculums test the ingenuity of everyone concerned with the teaching-learning process. Teachers who cannot re-educate themselves to accept new children and to adjust to cultural differences of children necessarily fail to meet the needs of the individual child. Some evidence indicates that teachers from middle-class cultures are not understood by children from less favored cultures. Certainly, evidence has indicated such children do not respond to middle-class culture-devised tests as do children from middle- or upper-class homes.[17]

All of the fifty states have had important changes in school enrollments during the past decade, and many of these have had very large increases. Five states have noted an increase in public school enrollment (between 1951–52 and 1961–62) in excess of 100 per cent. Alaska, a state with one of the smallest populations, has had an increase of 164 per cent; Florida, Nevada, California, and Arizona have all had an increase of public school enrollment of 102 per cent or more.[18]

A large per cent of the nation's teachers do not get their post-high school education in their home town. Colleges and universities wherein teachers are educated typically attract their students from many states. It is not unusual for such institutions to enroll students from every state in the nation and from foreign countries. Although some of these teachers return to their own communities, many do not. Some go on to teach in communities where the cultural back-

[17] Kenneth Eells, Allison Davis, Robert J. Havighurst, Virgil Herrick, and Ralph Tyler, *Intelligence and Cultural Differences* (Chicago: University of Chicago Press, 1951), pp. 1–371.

[18] National Education Association, *Ranking of the States* (Washington, D.C.: The Association, 1962), p. 17.

ground of the people is distinctly different from that to which the teachers had been accustomed. Others are recruited by school superintendents or other employing personnel in nearby states. All these situations require carefully planned in-service education programs if the nation's schools are to meet the needs of the people.

CHAPTER III

Methods of In-Service Education

Change and progress have been characteristic throughout this nation's history. How to make new knowledge available to others is one of the schools' greatest challenges. The addition of new ways of acquiring knowledge adds to the schools' responsibility for a continuing in-service education program. The newer methods of in-service education are many. One of the older ways of improving teaching was through "directing" teachers by the "authority" of the school. This ultimately emerged into supervision.

Changing Patterns of Supervision

Supervision in this country dates back to the time when the New England town meetings convened to pass judgment upon teachers and evaluate student learning. Its early history was distinctly unlike that of supervision today. It began at a time when subject matter to be memorized was specific and detailed. It was not until well into this century that somewhat radical changes in the nature of supervision took place. Paralleling this change was an improved understanding of the ways children develop, and the ways in which their intelligence, emotional behavior, and motivation differ. At the same time, the curriculum was greatly expanded, and the purposes of education were growing more complex. Under these circumstances it became apparent that the older forms of supervision were not meeting the needs of teachers and children.

Fred C. Ayer has traced the several stages or cycles of supervision from "inspection and improvement of classroom teaching" to an emphasis on "creativity" and "democratic leadership" and even later to an increase of emphasis on "better human relations." [1]

---

[1] Fred C. Ayer, *Fundamentals of Instructional Supervision* (New York: Harper & Row, Publishers, 1954), pp. 5, 6.

Supervision Shifts Emphasis to Growth of People

The recent shift of emphasis in supervision is important. The improvement of instruction is a byproduct of this new emphasis and purpose. New knowledge made available from studies in psychology and sociology as well as from studies in education currently place emphasis on the total circumstances including, primarily, the people involved that encourage learning.

An increasing amount of evidence clearly indicates that the educational growth of the professional staff is greater when democratic principles are understood and used. With all of the known ways of in-service education none can supplant that of teachers finding their own problems and working to find their own answers. Such a program of in-service education does not preclude the necessity for a supervisor. It does necessitate a philosophy of education that is based upon an understanding of human nature and the way we learn, and freedom to explore.

Understanding the Purpose of Supervision

It is important that the general purpose of supervision be clearly understood by the entire professional staff of a school system. Through the past forty years a great volume of literature dealing with supervision has been published. It is evident that supervisors themselves have been exploring to find the most effective role they could play in improving teaching and learning. As indicated above, much of supervision has been that of the supervisor telling or directing or demonstrating in order to help the teacher learn more about controlling and directing students toward better learning. This has been an important function. Through these years the subject matter to be learned has been expanded considerably, and a substantial amount of experimentation and research has added to our knowledge about child growth and development.

As expanded subject matter and increased knowledge of how children learn have been made available to supervisors and leaders in education, it has appeared that teachers have had greater needs for the help that could be provided by those designated to supervise. Consequently, supervision, in all of its history, has been regarded as a most effective means of in-service education. The speed of change, described in Chapter II, has increased the need for effective supervision.

Considerable evidence indicates that many school systems have changed their purposes of supervision very little. Under such circumstances, the supervisor continues to "instruct" teachers on methods of teaching. The emphasis in such schools is placed upon the ability of the supervisor, through his observation of classroom procedure, to detect the problems that need solution. Conferences are held between supervisor and teacher, generally with an understanding that the supervisor has the answers to the problems.

An improved method of supervision, supported by research, would adhere to a philosophy of education in which all of the professional personnel of a school system understand that knowledge has accumulated so rapidly in recent years that no one person can possibly know all that he needs to know as a professional person, and consequently he must have help from others and, in turn, share his knowledge with his colleagues.

The supervisor's role then becomes that of a facilitator, a person who sets the stage for the complex act of people growing together.

The shift of emphasis from "directing" teachers to studying teacher needs and establishing a climate that will be conducive to growth marks a wide departure from earlier supervisory responsibilities.

Mildred E. Swearingen suggests that the three principal duties of the supervisor are: (1) to determine teacher needs, (2) to establish cooperative action in attempts to solve problems, and (3) to work for a sensitivity to change.[2]

Reba M. Burnham states that supervisors must change their older methods of working with teachers if they are to remain effective.[3] Suggestions are made by which supervisors may develop the skills needed for newer roles such as through (1) "internships," conducted by a college or university, in which the "internee" would have contact with both the school system and the higher institution,

---

[2] Mildred E. Swearingen, "Identifying Needs for In-Service Growth," *Educational Leadership*, Vol. XVII, No. 6 (March, 1960), 332–35.

[3] Reba M. Burnham, "In-Service Education of Supervisors," *Educational Leadership*, Vol. XIX, No. 2 (November, 1961), 103–106.

(2) "seminars in geographical areas" in which supervisors in a particular portion of a state would participate, and (3) "weekend seminars."

The Role of the Supervisor
in Changing Teacher Behavior

If the supervisor is to be a leader in education, he must be sensitive to change and must initiate new and challenging programs. His sensitivity to change must include an awareness of the new purposes of education and an understanding of the role of education in American life.

Specifically, the supervisor can assist in the changing of teacher behavior by:

1. Helping teachers to identify new problems;
2. Assisting teachers in examining and selecting new objectives of education;
3. Cooperating with teachers in various research or group study programs;
4. Encouraging added creativity and originality;
5. Extending praise and confidence for venturesome investigations;
6. Supporting and sustaining teachers, especially beginning teachers;
7. Providing curriculum materials and other possible innovations, such as teaching machines and programmed learning materials, for experimental purposes;
8. Assisting teachers in preparing and using evaluating criteria;
9. Listening with empathy and understanding to teacher problems;
10. Building comfortable relations among teachers, between teachers and students, between teachers and other members of the professional staff, and between teachers and the public;
11. Suggesting possible methods of in-service education between teachers and education provided by higher institutions (such as university-sponsored workshops, and educational travel tours);
12. Eliminating threatening experiences and encouraging diverse opinions and teaching behavior;
13. Planning with teachers on programs of intraschool visiting;
14. Encouraging and supporting teachers in professional association activities;
15. Bridging any (undesirable) gap between teachers and administration;
16. Coordinating efforts of research or other study groups to avoid duplication of effort;
17. Making available important research findings to teachers;
18. Holding individual teacher conferences when and where needed;

19. Encouraging community activity and membership in nonprofessional associations;
20. Evaluating the effectiveness of the total supervisory program.

In summary, it may be said that supervision is needed because modern education has become extremely complex. Education is and should be making rapid changes. Much is now known concerning high quality education and this knowledge should be pooled and shared by all teachers. New investigations by teacher groups should be continuous in an endless quest for truth. The total professional staff of a given school or of a school system must work together to assure personal and group growth.

No one in a school system has greater need for in-service education than the supervisor. Some plans in operation show great promise for promoting the growth of those in this role.[4] These include cooperative programs with universities, internships in which the supervisor is paid by the school system but works closely with the higher institution (perhaps under its leadership), seminars in particular state and geographical areas, institutes dedicated to finding solutions to general problems, and regular curriculum research institutes.[5]

The Workshop as a Means of In-Service Education

The first regularly organized educational activity designated a "workshop," according to Alonzo F. Myers, "was conducted at Ohio State University in 1936."[6] By 1951 the workshop, as a device of in-service education, had extended all over the United States and had spread to foreign lands.[7]

Gertrude H. Hildreth has said a workshop can mean "almost anything from a series of field trips or a scientific expedition to intensive study of educational problems."[8]

The very wide use of the term *workshop* may be noted by a re-

[4] *Ibid.*
[5] *Ibid.*
[6] Alonzo F. Myers, "Workshops," *The Journal of Educational Sociology,* Vol. 24, No. 5 (January, 1951), 249.
[7] Walter A. Anderson, "What Makes a Good Workshop," *The Journal of Educational Sociology,* Vol. 24, No. 5 (June, 1951), 251.
[8] Gertrude H. Hildreth, "Evaluation of a Workshop in Education," *Teachers College Record,* Vol. 46 (February, 1945), 310.

view of the literature: "The workshop continues to be the most popular form of in-service education. Over 200 articles dealing with the workshop were reviewed in preparing this chapter." [9]

The workshop has certain characteristics that make it a valuable means of in-service education. Among these are the following:

1. It emerges to meet the existing needs of the participants;
2. It provides expert assistance (commonly from higher institutions);
3. It is flexible and consequently can be adapted to many diverse groups and situations;
4. It provides for the pooling of information and sharing of experiences;
5. It motivates participants to change their behavior where and when such changes may be helpful;
6. It gives added support to a changing program by assuring approval of the group;
7. It develops both individual and group skills in attacking new problems;
8. It adds morale to a faculty or a school system;
9. It strengthens working relations with others in different status assignments;
10. It develops knowhow in utilizing democratic procedures in other situations (such as teachers working with students);
11. It redefines and refines the objectives of education;
12. It evaluates both the results of the effort and the process by which results are attained.

Certain situations or conveniences appear to enhance the success of the workshop. Among these are the following:

1. Appropriate physical conditions for group action (meetings may be successful if held out of doors or at least at some distance from the school);
2. Availability of consultants where and when assistance is needed;
3. Assistance of a secretary-recorder with paper, pencils, and such items that may be needed by participants;
4. Access to bibliographies dealing with the problem of major concern;
5. Access to library facilities.

A successful workshop is more easily described than defined. It

---

[9] J. Cecil Parker and William P. Golden, Jr., "In-Service Education of Elementary- and Secondary-School Teachers," *Review of Educational Research*, Vol. 22, No. 3 (June, 1952), 193.

is the process which is most important. Successful workshops frequently terminate with the production of materials of various kinds deemed to be important in teaching. If production of curriculum materials were the sole objective, however, these could be prepared by a curriculum director or as a result of his directions to others who may produce such materials. Such alternative procedures, however, frequently do not bring about changes in teacher behavior.

Workshops emphasize informality, and establish good rapport and interrelatedness. That people do enjoy workshops may be noted by the frequency with which they attend. Although a possible danger of some waste of time exists when the program is not highly structured, participants generally become highly active and learn to do by doing.

Teaching is living and working toward the optimum growth of everyone concerned. It is essentially a process of interrelating as students and teachers extend themselves toward ever-expanding goals. Its success depends largely upon the way each individual relates to each other individual. Frank E. Allen has declared that a major value emerging from the workshop method of in-service education is in the human relations aspect.[10]

Interinstitutional Programs for In-Service Education

The individual's educational growth is or should be a continuous process. It begins at birth and extends throughout his life. Schools are institutions created by society to enhance the growth of its members. Colleges or universities have neither a greater nor a lesser responsibility to the individual than do schools below the college level. In other words, although the administration and other aspects of the institutions differ, the purpose of all schools is to help people achieve educational growth.

Many public schools and colleges have had years of experience in cooperating in this common purpose. Perhaps the clearest example of such cooperation in student teaching is that of the thousands of prospective teachers who spend a portion of a year

---

[10] Frank E. Allen, "In-Service Education," *Nation's Schools,* Vol. 48, No. 3 (September, 1951), 45.

observing and teaching in the public schools while working under the joint supervision of the school system and the college.

One common cooperative procedure is for colleges and universities to "follow" the young teacher after graduation and give assistance as it may be needed.

The public schools—students, teachers, and facilities—are frequently used by higher institutions for experimental and other purposes. Hundreds of study meetings are held annually that involve teachers from all levels of all educational institutions. Teachers look to higher institutions for advanced training of diverse kinds. Many current cooperative programs are designed to award a master's degree (after a fifth year of training) as evidence of the teacher's becoming a master teacher. One such program is the Oberlin College program for a Master of Arts in Teaching.[11] Initiated by Oberlin, it is now being adopted by other institutions. The plan "seeks to provide a balanced course of study consisting of (1) advanced work in the student's major and related fields, (2) basic courses in education, and (3) student teaching in the form of internship." [12]

One of the most important developments of teacher education during the past decade has been the widening array of graduate courses (often with scholarships) offered by colleges and universities. This device has been particularly noticeable in the fields of mathematics and science. The attempt has been to improve the quality of teaching in the secondary schools by improving teacher competence in the subject matter they teach. One successful approach by universities, according to Randall M. Whaley, has been that of awarding "a Master of Arts degree in teaching with specific emphasis on subject matter and by the offering of summer and academic-year institutes. . . ." [13]

A number of higher institutions during recent years have initiated

---

[11] Andreas M. Kazamias, "The Education of Good Teachers and the Oberlin Master of Arts in Teaching Program," *Journal of Teacher Education,* Vol. XII, No. 2 (June, 1962), 205–208.

[12] *Ibid.,* pp. 206, 207.

[13] Randall M. Whaley, "Graduate Education for Teachers," in *The Education of Teachers: New Perspectives.* Report of the Second Bowling Green Conference (Washington, D.C.: National Commission on Teacher Education and Professional Standards, National Education Association, 1948), p. 330.

special degrees intended to encourage advanced study by avoiding the rigid routine of specified requirements characteristic of the older traditional degrees. One such is the Specialist in Education degree, or Ed. S.[14]

Also, some institutions, such as the East Central State College of Ada, Oklahoma, award a Degree of Master of Teaching, a fifth-year program.[15]

A program worthy of note is the University of Wisconsin Plan for Teacher Education, in which other colleges and/or departments cooperate.[16] This plan is a cooperative all-institution approach. It is based upon the conviction that the training of teachers is so important that the entire university faculty must be involved in planning, teaching, and evaluating the program. For more than thirty years the School of Education of the University of Wisconsin has involved all departments which in any way contribute or participate in the training of teachers. Under this plan, therefore, in 1961–62 888 professors who represented 65 departments had direct concern with educating teachers. They had the responsibility of planning, teaching, evaluating, and otherwise participating in the total program of the School of Education.

The program's determined effort to improve quality may be noted by the fact that prospective teachers are required to maintain a grade point average higher than the minimum required by other departments in the university and by the requirement that "each department must certify those students who have qualified to be recommended for a license to teach." [17]

An increasingly common method of providing in-service education for graduate students working for advanced degrees is that of supervised internships. Such a program has been instituted by the

[14] Felix Robb, "Post-Graduate Development of Teaching Competence," *Teacher Education: The Decade Ahead* (Washington, D.C.: National Commission on Teacher Education and Professional Standards, National Education Association, 1955), p. 301.

[15] Charles F. Spencer, "East Central State College Program of Graduate Study for Teachers in Service," *Teacher Education: The Decade Ahead* (Washington, D.C.: National Commission on Teacher Education and Professional Standards, National Education Association, 1955), p. 335.

[16] Lindley J. Stiles, "The University of Wisconsin Plan for Teacher Education," *School and Society,* Vol. 90, No. 2209 (April, 1962), 189–91.

[17] *Ibid.,* p. 190.

University of Maryland,[18] where the advanced student (who has had teaching experience), under the supervision of the University, works with a superintendent or with some other person in an administrative or other technical position.

Summer Schools

As the demands for advanced education of teachers have increased, colleges and universities have consistently added to their summer programs. It is now nearly universal practice in the United States for higher institutions to include the summer session as a regular part of the academic offering. One purpose of the summer school is to shorten the time required for the regularly enrolled student to obtain the bachelor's degree. Another major reason for the summer session is and has been that of enabling teachers to further their training toward an advanced degree. That teachers are conspicuous on university campuses during the summer may be noted by the greater maturity of summer school students as compared with that of students during the regular academic year.

Announcements of summer school offerings are regularly made in the educational literature. These offerings are so extensive and include so many kinds of courses that one report appropriately states: "Almost an endless list of opportunities exists this year to attend summer programs of the nation's institutions of higher education." [19]

University Extension Programs

The National University Extension Association was organized in 1915 and since that time has played an important role in the education and re-education of many people. It is one of the major sources of in-service education for teachers. During the years of critical shortages of teachers since World War II, scores of university extension divisions have done much to help teachers obtain certification and at the same time to equip them with the added knowledge needed for successful teaching.

---

[18] Clarence A. Newell and Richard H. Byrne, "Field Experience in Education," *The Journal of Teacher Education*, Vol. X, No. 4 (December, 1959), 435–38.
[19] *School and Society*, Vol. 77 (April, 1953), 246–47; (May, 1953), 280–82.

At the thirty-fifth annual meeting of the National University Association, a study concerned with "the needs that gave rise to institutional arrangements for off-campus study" reported for 45 of 54 colleges and institutions that had land-grant status. Of the total number reporting, 24 indicated that "the need for in-service training of educational personnel was a principal factor in the demand for off-campus study arrangements." [20]

Institutes

Since the enactment of the National Defense Education Act, a considerable variety of institutes and other study programs have been held to serve as devices for the in-service training of teachers. As the result of this Act, 37 institutes were held during the summer of 1960. The evaluation team appointed by the United States Office of Education said these were ". . . a dynamic and positive achievement. They gave some two thousand modern languages teachers unprecedented experience. . . . They contributed toward meeting the rapidly increasing demand for better trained, more competent secondary school and grade school teachers of modern language." [21]

The National Defense Language Development Program Title VI provides for the training of teachers in foreign languages. A description of this program stated: "With an appropriation of $15,630,000 for two years of operation, the Language Development Program has arranged for the conduct of 58 institutes for 3169 elementary teachers. . . ." [22]

The United States Commissioner of Education "awarded National Defense modern foreign language fellowships to 474 graduate students for study during the 1960–61 academic year. Federal appropriations for the language fellowship program totaled $1,550,000." [23]

---

[20] F. C. Lowry, "Evaluation of Graduate Work Offered by Land-Grant Institutions Through Off-Campus Study Arrangements," *National University Extension Association, Proceedings,* Vol. 33 (May, 1950), 51.

[21] Stephen A. Freeman, "An Evaluation of the 1960 Summer Language Institute," *The Modern Language Journal,* Vol. XLV, No. 3 (March, 1961), 105.

[22] *The Modern Language Journal,* Vol. XLV, No. 2 (February, 1961), 102.

[23] *The Modern Language Journal,* Vol. XLV, No. 1 (January, 1961), 52.

Title VI of the Act states:

> The Commissioner of Education is authorized to contract with
> U. S. institutions of higher education for the operation of institutes
> which provide advanced training to teachers, supervisors, or train-
> ers of teachers of modern languages in elementary or secondary
> schools. . . . The Government pays all operating costs of such
> institutes, and each public school teacher who participates may ap-
> ply for a stipend of $75 per week, plus an allowance of $15 per
> week for each dependent, for the duration of his attendance.[24]

The institutes include teachers of Spanish, French, German, Rus-
sian, Italian, Hebrew, Chinese, and Japanese.

The Commissioner of Education is also authorized to award fellowships in designated languages and in related studies needed for
a full understanding of the area, region, or country in which such
languages are commonly spoken. Such study must be at a United
States institution of higher education offering appropriate graduate
instruction.[25]

Short-term intensive institutes have been found to have considerable value as a means of in-service education. One example of such
an institute was the six-week general science institute sponsored by
the National Science Foundation at the University of Pennsylvania
during the summer of 1959. Tests were administered at the beginning and end of the six-week period to determine the gain achieved
during this time. Fowler claims "a very significant gain" was noted.[26]

The institute has during recent years become a common device for
adding to the teacher's knowledge and is used in many areas of academic learning. These intensive courses are financed by the federal
government, and by various independent foundations, industrial
corporations, and universities. The educational literature reports a
wide array of scholarships and fellowships that are available from
time to time.[27]

---

[24] "Notes and News," *The Modern Language Journal*, Vol. XLV, No. 7 (November, 1961), 322.

[25] *Ibid.*

[26] H. Seymour Fowler, "Evaluation of An Institute for the Training of Elementary-School Science Resource Teachers," *Journal of Educational Research*, Vol.
53, No. 9 (May, 1960), 358–59.

[27] As an example, note *The Modern Language Journal*, Vol. XLV, No. 6 (October, 1961), 254.

School Study Councils

No one has a greater need for in-service education than persons in administrative positions. Various means have been attempted to provide status leaders with added training. One device which is growing in popularity is the school study council.

Twenty years ago, Paul Mort initiated the first school study council of consequence in the United States. Mort's concern had arisen because of the lag between the recognition of needs in education and the utilization of existing knowledge to meet these needs. The objective of this council was to bring together the knowledge and skill of administrative personnel and to share this knowledge with other council members. It soon became apparent that this was an excellent device for school administrators, and the plan spread. The council usually works closely with the college or university with which it is affiliated. A university faculty member serves as a consultant, but the council has its own plan of organization and its own officers.

Council members study problems of challenge and common interest. Although procedures differ some from council to council, many hold study meetings four or more times during the school year and devote most of a day to each problem.

In-Service Education
Through Professional Associations

The absence of any central agency for the control of education in the United States and the traditional freedom of the states and local school districts to direct their own education permits unusual diversity in teaching. It also permits professional associations to influence the training of teachers.

The National Education Association, largest of these associations and—in a sense—the parent of many others, is composed of people engaged in education but with diverse interests and backgrounds. During its more than one hundred years of existence, it has made important contributions to the educational growth of many thousands of teachers. It has attained its present status through the growth of its membership, which is entirely voluntary.

There are many other smaller education associations. Associations of superintendents, secondary-school principals, elementary-school principals, classroom teachers, supervisors, curriculum directors, adult educators, and others all have their headquarters in the National Education Association headquarters. In a sense these associations are part of the larger association, but they maintain their own elected officers to develop programs for those who regularly work in a specific capacity in a state or local school system. Each of the states has an educational association that is affiliated with the National Education Association and serves on the state level in much the same capacity that the larger association does on a national level.

Other professional associations—such as Phi Delta Kappa, Delta Kappa Gamma, and the Association for Childhood Education International—are not an organic part of the National Education Association, but fill a similar function in developing publications and holding professional meetings for their respective members.

Teachers of mathematics, English, social studies, and other subject-matter areas have national associations, hold annual meetings for their membership, and publish printed information that is sent through the mail.

Many professional educators may have membership in more than one of these associations. Each year large numbers of teachers meet in national, regional, state, and local conventions for the primary purpose of improving their abilities and adding to their knowledge as professional people. The number of people in educational service attending such meetings each year has not been precisely determined, but it is known to be large.

A study made by the Research Division of the National Education Association in 1957–58 revealed that "four out of five eligible persons belong to their local association" and that "a wide range of activities is carried on: business meetings, lectures, workshops, newsletters, social activities, and work for legislation affecting education." [28]

In addition to providing person-to-person contacts among mem-

---

[28] *NEA Research Bulletin,* Vol. 38, No. 2 (May, 1960), 41.

bers at their meetings, the educational associations publish large quantities of informational material. This total professional association effort to help teachers grow professionally is a most interesting phenomenon.

CHAPTER IV

Contributions of Research
to In-Service Education

This is an age of research. We seek the newest and latest style or model of all of our material possessions. It is as if it were a social stigma to be out of date. Our greatest effort has been directed toward increasing our material possessions. The obvious possession—that which can be seen by others—appears to be more glamorous whether on an individual or national level. World conditions and the development of a highly competitive capitalistic economy—the success of which is dependent upon change and progress—have made research and scientific investigation take on connotations that appear to be very important in our society. In fact, we have come to think of an ability to conduct research as an important characteristic of an educated person. Research is particularly emphasized at the graduate level of the university. Many believe that the quality of a college or university may be measured largely by the amount of research that is pursued by the faculty. In fact, some institutions employ scholars, not to teach, but only to conduct research.

Basic Research: A Search for Truth

The front page of almost any newspaper contains news that has the characteristics of both pure and applied science. The federal government (substantially the largest supporter of research in the nation) is employing able scientists who are working in pure or basic science. For example, the government is eager to find out more and more about nuclear power in this space age. But the government is also concerned with finding applications for this newly-discovered knowledge. It is in these two areas and the interrelation between them that we have developed our technology. We have become more aware of the implications of applied science as we have seen and experienced its benefits in our daily lives.

The terms *pure or basic science* or *laboratory research* may be frightening to many teachers, but they need not be. Perhaps most teachers will not indulge in carefully controlled experiments, but some will and probably more should. It is an effective method of in-service education, and it has been responsible for much of what we know about child growth and development. As already indicated, there is much, indeed, that we need to know in these areas that can be determined only by careful experimentation. Teachers are in the best possible position to study children because they are with them daily. Given freedom to explore, teachers can establish their own research designs and conduct their own experiments.

Many of the conclusions reached by other experimentors need verification from classroom teachers. Teachers, under certain circumstances, may be too quick to accept what others have pronounced as truth.

We probably would not have moved very far from the use of the hornbook or the method of teaching reading by first teaching the alphabet had it not been for a vast amount of research and experimentation by individuals who were motivated to find new answers to old problems. The individual teacher is in a unique position to develop experimental programs focused on student learning and the curriculum. Emphasis at this point is placed upon effort by the individual teacher because teaching is so complex that variables caused by differences between teachers are difficult to control. Individual teachers have made significant research findings in such subject-matter areas as reading, arithmetic, and spelling. Other teachers, working alone, have made important research contributions leading to a better understanding of children.

Research by Individual Teachers: A Point of View

We depend on science and research for progress and for the general improvement of living. Teachers need to have a research point of view. They need to be able to establish a research design for studying some of their unsolved problems, and they need to know the methods by which they may pursue such investigations. As late as 1957, McKim said: "Only a start has been made in helping teachers to become research-minded." [1]

A major difference between a trade and a profession is that the tradesman makes little change in his methods from day to day or from year to year, while, on the other hand, a major characteristic of most professions is their tendency to change. This is particularly true in education. The schools cannot meet their responsibility without changing.

The role of research as an integral part of in-service education is not only to find new truths or new and better ways of doing what needs to be done for the improvement of education, but also to help teachers take a more objective point of view toward teaching procedures. During the years that critics of the schools have been increasingly vocal, there has been some danger that teachers would tend to defend their existing programs rather than search for improvement through research.

In order to bring about progress and needed change, it is necessary for all teachers to be imaginative and exploratory. Without this motivating characteristic, civilization would be in danger of deterioration. The belief that cultures remain unchanged over generations is a myth in spite of the fact that those which neglect research change little. Man, by his very nature, is equipped to produce change. He possesses drives that appear never to be satisfied, but endlessly impel him to find more and new satisfactions.

Stinnott [2] has shown that great teaching (at any level) involves motivating the learner to enter realms of unknown experiences. He maintains that people "as living organisms are bound to seek goals." He says: "They cannot help it, for such is the nature of life itself." [3]

Stinnott comes directly to the point:

> Man's questing heritage is more than simply seeking to reach those goals that the experience of the race has shown to be satisfy-

---

[1] Margaret G. McKim, "Curriculum Research in Historical Perspective," Association for Supervision and Curriculum Development, *1957 Yearbook* (Washington, D.C.: National Education Association, 1957), p. 38.

[2] Edmund W. Stinnott, "The Questing Heritage," in *The Nature of Being Human,* Marie I. Rasey, ed. (Detroit, Mich.: Wayne State University Press, 1959).

[3] *Ibid.,* p. 19.

ing. Man is an explorer, a frontiersman, an adventurer who is continually seeking to push out into new and undiscovered territory.[4]

The Need for Understanding the Characteristics of Research

Any effective in-service education program must be concerned with finding new and better ways of changing the behavior of school children and adding to the knowledge or skill of the teacher-researcher. Only a small part of the 1.5 million teachers of the United States is engaged in serious research. The term *research* is loosely used and is erroneously applied to any teacher-assigned activity from a third-grade child copying a statement from a reference book to the efforts of a few teachers who are using scientific procedures to seek truth not yet within the realm of human knowledge.

The purpose of research that may be classified as scientific is to discover truth, to understand cause and effect relationship, and to make accurate prediction. Research involves:

1. Recognizing a problem;
2. Establishing an hypothesis;
3. Surveying all related data that shed light on the problem;
4. Pursuing the hypothesis to a conclusion (preferably by carefully controlled experimentation);
5. Arriving at a conclusion (one may possibly deviate from this source or terminate the study on the basis of findings);
6. Making a generalization for application and/or establishing a principle.

If instruction in research methods is not included in the teacher's preparatory education, his in-service education should include some usable information to improve his research skill. An objective, analytical, and unbiased approach to the solution of educational problems is necessary for teaching success. Each teacher should learn how to establish and use an hypothesis, at least in an elementary fashion. (Good, Barr, and Scates state an hypothesis is merely a "tentative inference as to the existence of some fact.")[5]

The existing cultural climate of the nation, with its reliance on

[4] *Ibid.*, p. 24.

[5] Carter V. Good, A. S. Barr, and Douglas E. Scates, *The Methodology of Educational Research* (New York: Appleton-Century-Crofts, Inc. 1941), p. 185.

science, should permeate the classrooms. An attitude of inquiry and an eagerness for an expansion of knowledge serve as the basis for all learning. This appears to be as true in the social sciences as in the exact sciences.[6]

Research in education is not a new phenomenon. Its importance increased with the use of tests and measurements developed early in this century and with the use of scientific procedures by scholars in the behavioral sciences. Although much was written concerning educational research during the 1920's, Carter Good's book, *How to Do Research in Education,*[7] was among the first publications to describe clearly the use of scientific investigation in education.

Although the so-called science of education appeared important with the introduction of intelligence tests and other kinds of objective measurements during and after World War I, it appears to be only since World War II that a new awareness has developed requiring more scientific study of all kinds of human relations (including teacher-teacher and teacher-student relations).

Teachers, particularly those with a zest for exploration, ought not to fear either the terminology or the method of science. They are in a position to formulate new concepts and to discern new cause and effect relationships. May Brodleck writes:

> Scientists . . . formulate concepts with which to describe the facts they find. They look for laws connecting some of these facts with others. They try to formulate theories in order to explain known facts and laws to help find new ones.[8]

Teachers can learn to follow this procedure.

The Individual Teacher and Research

The typical teacher considers himself a practitioner, not a researcher. His educational experience preparatory to teaching was largely a combination of listening to lectures and reading, all of which add up to getting an education by "being told" by others.

---

[6] Neil Postman, "The Scientific Spirit and the Modern Classroom," *Teachers College Record,* Vol. 62, No. 1 (October, 1960), 299–303.

[7] Carter V. Good, *How to Do Research in Education* (Baltimore, Md.: Warwick and York, Inc., 1928), pp. 5–298.

[8] May Brodleck, "The Philosophy of Science and Educational Research," *Review of Educational Research,* Vol. XXVII, No. 5 (December, 1957), 427.

His student teaching and allied experiences involved observing teachers control and direct students through lecturing. Some studies indicate that teachers tend to teach as they were taught. However, colleges of education in recent years are encouraging prospective teachers to develop a more scientific point of view and to use such a point of view as a part of the teaching process.

In-service training programs should encourage teachers to develop a scientific method for their own use and as a method in teaching. Although we live in an age characterized by science and research, it is also an age of fiction, mysticism, and propaganda. The teacher, therefore, should help students to become objective, critical, and reasonably free from the prejudices that impair honest thinking. Research has repeatedly proved that quality teaching involves using a problem-solving approach.[9]

In their search for improvement, teachers at all levels could increase their effectiveness if they would adopt the approach described by Gaylord P. Harnwell, president of the University of Pennsylvania:

> This implies a highly motivated effort, a striving for what as yet is unattained, an initiative in attack, an ingenuity in method, an imaginative approach to the unknown, a skepticism of what is unclear or undemonstrable, and a readiness to recognize and admit whim and vagary and error.[10]

The United States Congress has indicated its interest in research by several legislative acts. One such was that which in 1954 created the Cooperative Research Program, enabling the United States Office of Education to conduct research in cooperation with state departments of public instruction and with colleges and universities. This program helps to meet some of the existing needs for more research in which the federal government may be involved.[11]

Many segments of the teaching profession recognize the need for more research. The American Educational Research Association

---

[9] Many sources of information dealing with "research design" are available. One such is Marie Jahoda, Morton Deutsch, and Stuart W. Cook, *Research Methods in Social Relations* (New York: The Dryden Press, 1951), Part I, Chap. 3.

[10] Gaylord P. Harnwell, "Signposts for American Higher Education," *School and Society,* Vol. 90, No. 2211 (Summer, 1962), 256.

[11] Lindley J. Stiles, "The Cooperative Research Program," *Phi Delta Kappan,* Vol. XLIII, No. 6 (March, 1962), 231–36.

(National Education Association), the Research Division of the National Education Association, and the Association for Supervision and Curriculum Development (National Education Association), are examples of professional associations devoted to research.

Phi Delta Kappa has regarded research in education as one of its three major goals. In December, 1961, the president of this association declared that it was its intent to develop new methods of bringing research to the teachers and administrators. Moreover, he declared the leaders of education "must find a way to establish large-scale educational research." [12]

The platform of the National Education Association declares: "Education, like all professions, is a service based on research. . . ." [13]

The Educational Policies Commission has maintained that it is "the business of every professional" to contribute to the total knowledge of the teaching profession through research.[14]

There are a number of reasons why most teachers should be conducting research.[15] Involvement in research requires a careful study of the literature associated with a proposed research problem and serves as excellent motivation for extensive and critical reading. It compels the researcher to think through and establish a workable research design. It forces the teacher to develop a scientific attitude, an attitude of objectivity and scholarship. It motivates the teacher to make generalizations and applications from research findings, and helps him perceive the implications of and possible solutions for related problems and situations. It compels a blending of humility and scholarship that is an asset to any teacher. It creates a climate of scholarship that is important to any faculty or school system. It impels the teacher to make a written (and often an oral) description of the research process. It extends the spectrum of interests. It is a major means of receiving deserved recognition. It assists a teacher to learn what he did not know before and often to

---

[12] Charles R. Foster, "Current Challenges to Educational Leadership," *Phi Delta Kappan,* Vol. XLIII, No. 3 (December, 1961), 108.

[13] National Education Association, *Addresses and Proceedings,* Ninety-ninth Annual Meeting, Vol. 99 (1961), 417.

[14] Educational Policies Commission, *Professional Organizations in American Education* (Washington, D.C.: National Education Association, 1957), p. 31.

[15] Byron G. Massialas and Frederick R. Smith, "Quality Research—A Goal for Every Teacher," *Phi Delta Kappan,* Vol. XLIII, No. 6 (March, 1962), 253–56.

discover in the process the uselessness and handicaps of his prejudices.

A noticeable increase of research has taken place during recent years. Most of this, however, is in universities, with a lesser amount in state departments of public instruction. Research grants from the federal government and from independent foundations have had an important influence on this trend. This increase is probably what motivated Clark and Carriker to declare: "By 1970 it may be possible to state that more was learned about education in the 1960's than had been learned in the previous history of education in this country." [16]

In spite of the publication of some early classic research dealing with teaching and learning and the use of this content in classes at the university level, the lag in applying these research findings has tended to continue. Consequently, it is maintained that educational practice has been changing too slowly and has not made use of this research. For some time social psychologists have been studying the behavior of groups and leaders in education have been at work at using their findings in developing programs of action research.

Action research generally is not the carefully controlled experimentation comparable to that carried on in laboratories, but it does have distinct advantages. Among these are the following:

1. It challenges the interests of several or many people;
2. It arises out of the recognized needs of one or more teachers;
3. It serves as a valuable means of enhancing the in-service education of teachers;
4. It has practical application for those who become engaged in it;
5. It has potential for changing the behavior of teachers toward improved teaching;
6. It builds morale;
7. It provides for more freedom to explore and apply new subject matter and new methods of teaching;
8. It improves channels of communication among the professional staff;
9. It involves administrators and supervisors as well as teachers in the process of seeking truth;
10. It involves or may involve lay people and thereby helps in the interpretation of the school program to the public;

---

[16] David L. Clark and William R. Carriker, "Educational Research and the Cooperative Research Program," *Phi Delta Kappan*, Vol. XLII, No. 6 (March, 1961), 226.

11. It improves teacher understanding of child growth;
12. It focuses attention on the creativity and imagination of teachers;
13. It serves as a model for teachers to use in classrooms;
14. It closes the gulf between knowledge and application;
15. It affords flexibility and is readily submitted to retesting or re-analysis;
16. It is the best-known way to effect needed changes in the curriculum.

Substantial evidence has been accumulated which indicates that most teachers change their methods of teaching very little after initial patterns or habits are established unless they develop a genuine desire to change. This desire appears not to develop sufficiently unless the teacher becomes involved in some action or process that involves change.

Action research has been particularly fruitful in areas of curriculum study, in developing improved methods of teaching (changing teacher behavior in the classroom), and in improving morale by freeing channels of communication from psychological blockings. It is now recognized to be one of the best means of in-service education.

No exacting framework exists within which action research must operate. It may involve two people or two hundred. It may involve a committee in search of an answer to a minor problem, or a large school system striving toward over-all improvement.

The innovations of action research as a means of curriculum improvement have indeed changed the course of study over the past thirty years or more. Teachers under the direction of administrators then "wrote" the course of study. This was essentially busy work and did little for those engaged in that procedure. Concern developed because neither teacher nor student behavior changed as a result of this effort.

The research of that time, in the main, was conducted in an artificial setting by one well-trained in research design but with little concern for the impact of his experimentation on improving the teaching-learning process.

Other values of action research are that the teacher is learning to work democratically with others, that he is probably undergoing a continuous change in his understanding of education, and that he is learning new and improved methods of evaluating his own teaching.

Action research helps the teacher to function more effectively. It opens up new vistas by permitting an interchange of ideas. It helps remove antiquated methods of teaching and changes the teacher's behavior as he chooses to change.

The "fully functioning self," as described by Kelley,[17] is in an excellent position to participate in action research. He is the individual who thinks well of himself and of others and has a stake in the results of those with whom he works. He does this openly and has less fear of error because his openness helps him to profit from his mistakes.

Action research and growth in teaching are closely related. Each is a process of expanding one's knowledge, making decisions, and communicating with others. Arthur L. Rautman said: "There can be no sharp line of demarcation . . . between research and teaching; the two processes are basically interdependent." [18]

Action Research and the Curriculum

The innovations that have developed from teacher-conducted action research have substantially altered the process of studying the curriculum. It is in this area that the contribution of action research is most apparent. The content of the curriculum at best changes slowly. Undoubtedly, because of legal statutes or other regulations, some schools teach subject matter that is obsolete.

One of the most serious shortcomings of older methods of curriculum study under which subject matter as content was planned and prescribed before a teacher had seen his class was found to be that such a plan may not be at all appropriate for the students. Hilda Taba has reminded us that "teachers cannot project curriculum units before learning to diagnose the needs of their students." [19]

Likewise, Laura Zirbes claims that the earlier curriculum devised

[17] Earl C. Kelley, "The Fully Functioning Self," *Perceiving, Behaving, Becoming: A New Focus on Education,* Association for Supervision and Curriculum Development, 1962 Yearbook (Washington, D.C.: National Education Association, 1962), Chap. 2.

[18] Arthur L. Rautman, "Using Educational Research in Improving Instruction," *Educational Leadership,* Vol. VII, No. 3 (December, 1949), 183.

[19] Hilda Taba, "Problem Identification," *Research for Curriculum Development,* Association for Supervision and Curriculum Development, 1957 Yearbook (Washington, D.C.: National Education Association, 1957), p. 62.

by specialists or single experimentalists "was found to be too fixed and inflexible in the light of changing conditions." [20]

The curriculum that evolves from action research requires insight and knowledge about individual children. Judgment and choices must be used based upon that knowledge.

Careful studies of their behavior and their feelings about changing indicate that teachers derive added satisfaction from involvment in curriculum study. Corey has indicated this concern: "Learning that changes behavior substantially is most likely to result when a person himself tries to improve a situation that makes a difference to him." [21]

The great need for teacher growth and for a continuously modern curriculum requires that many more teachers become involved at the scene of their work. The pooling of information in terms of content to be taught is important, but much more important are the benefits derived from the involvement of teachers in their total school program. This tends to assure change in the needed direction and consequently is very rewarding as a means of in-service education.

---

[20] Laura Zirbes, "Our Research Responsibilities," *Educational Leadership*, Vol. IX, No. 8 (May, 1952), 486.

[21] Stephen M. Corey, *Action Research to Improve School Practices* (New York: Teachers College, Bureau of Publications, Columbia University, 1953), p. 9.

CHAPTER V

Organizing, Developing, and Evaluating In-Service Education

More than a century ago school trustees in a comparatively rural America were becoming convinced that education had reached a point of maturing that required leadership with some professional training. This decision, spreading as it did, gave birth to the offices of superintendent and principal. These officers, appointed by the trustees (later, by the boards of education), have maintained an important responsibility for the quality of teaching through the intervening decades. As education has come to play an increasingly important role in American life, the work of the administrative and supervisory personnel has increased in complexity. We are now at a time when real concern is expressed over ways of finding improved methods of making more rapid progress in quality education. This need for improvement appears to be general and is present in every aspect of the schools.

The Role of Administrative and Supervisory Personnel in In-Service Education

The superintendent of schools is in a unique position in the development and improvement of education. He is the professional staff's spokesman to the board of education and, in turn, the board's executive officer supervising the total professional staff.

Educational programs have so greatly expanded during recent years that the superintendent has necessarily become deeply involved in many phases of school duties not immediately concerned with the quality of teaching. The American Association of School Administrators,[1] other professional associations, and scholars take the point of view that this responsibility of the superintendent for

---

[1] American Association of School Administrators, *The Superintendent As Instructional Leader*, Thirty-Fifth Yearbook (Washington, D.C.: The Association, 1957), pp. 1–222.

the continuous improvement of teaching is a duty that cannot completely be delegated to others. It is the school board's right and duty to know (and to give approval) of the programs underway at any time which are intended to change or otherwise enhance the quality of teaching, and it is the duty of the superintendent to keep the board informed on this major item.

Any in-service education program directed by or toward the professional staff must be a part of the concerns of the superintendent. The superintendent of schools may or may not initiate the in-service education program, but he should be on the team that does initiate it and he must nourish a climate in which it may grow. He should be a part of the planning, the learning, and the evaluating. Similar roles should be played by all administrative and supervisory personnel. In-service education is for every one of the staff—none can afford to be exempt from learning.[2]

Individual superintendents differ and consequently see their duties differently. The insecure, poorly prepared administrator will most often operate a school based on traditional notions of authority. In such a school one may find experiences threatening to teachers and to children. It appears that every society of which there is a record has tended to use threats as a means of control. Such threats have characterized leaders of nations, leaders of households, administrators of schools, and teachers of classes. Children and adults have been told what to do and how and when to do it. This authoritarian climate is all too common in schools today. Fear of the consequences if one does or does not is a psychological weapon that has been universally used to whip people into an acceptance of the mores and into conformity. The administrator who supervises the teacher, like the teacher who supervises the student, reassures himself of his authority by exerting it.

The responsibility of the school superintendent as an instructional leader was expressed in the 1959 Yearbook of the American Association of School Administrators:

> As leader of the instructional program, the superintendent must be an educational expert. He should be a student of school practices

---

[2] For further analysis, see *In-Service Education,* The Fifty-Sixth Yearbook of the National Society for the Study of Education, Part I, Nelson B. Henry, ed. (Chicago: University of Chicago Press, 1957), Chaps. VI, VII.

and procedures and a scholar of America's cultural heritage and development. His function might be described as that of educational interpreter for the future as well as for the present and past.[3]

In-service education of teachers requires careful planning and a great deal of action and effort on the part of those who are responsible for the quality of the educational program. Thoughtful scholars agree that the superintendent of schools cannot shirk this duty, nor can he delegate to others certain inherent responsibilities for in-service education. All emphasize the absolute need for a sharing of responsibility among the entire staff; however, the initiation, the first forward push—although it may be suggested by another—must come from the executive of the board. Otherwise, he must relinquish the educational program to another.

The superintendent of schools should do the following:

1. Initiate, in cooperation with the staff, the tentative plan for an in-service educational program for all of the professional staff (and for others as needed);
2. Arrange with others the plan of work;
3. Help all participants to understand their responsibility and opportunity in the program;
4. Encourage action and build morale;
5. Agree upon a plan of work that places understandable and approved responsibility on status leaders;
6. Keep the board of education informed and provide facts to the interested public;
7. Express appreciation for meritorious effort;
8. Provide emotional support to participants;
9. Help structure research and study designs;
10. Analyze and evaluate research results;
11. Provide time for study groups as a part of the regular work of the professional staff;
12. Make available, when needed, consultant help;
13. Provide for publication of innovations that have a significant impact upon educational programs;
14. Make available physical facilities that are conducive to productive effort;
15. Make secretarial and related assistance available as needed.

The complex nature of a modern education program requires

---

[3] American Association of School Administrators, *Educational Administration in a Changing Community*, Thirty-Seventh Yearbook (Washington, D.C.: The Association, 1959), p. 125.

many kinds of skills and abilities. No individual, by any stretch of the imagination, can now have all the answers needed in such schools. It is this coworker concept that George Sharp was concerned with when he stated that the modern staff is composed of people "with differing abilities and training rather than a *gradation* of abilities and training ranging from inferior to superior." [4]

Background of Problems
Confronting the Administrator

The traditional concept of school organization and administration actually may be a means of retarding the growth of teachers, if the assumption is that the administrator was selected because he "knew" what was to be done—because he possessed "all" the answers. Laura Zirbes refers to such a school as one in which "conformity was expected" and teachers "who made good cogs were approved." She declares that these teachers "were the pride of principals and superintendents who ran the educational mills." [5]

Fortunately, these extremely rigid lines of autocracy are breaking down and the flow of authority is assuming a horizontal rather than vertical direction. Moreover, this is a two-way flow and, in the case of administration, is becoming a process of asking questions and suggesting possible answers rather than simply giving directives.

The authors of the School Administrators' 1957 Yearbook freely admit that the superintendent is confronted with a difficult job in his responsibility of using the group process as a means of improving instruction, and that this difficulty has several facets. They believe the superintendent or other status leaders are often inadequately trained to initiate and work with a group other than on the basis of a status leader. They also claim that the leader often lacks skill in using the scientific method in solving practical problems. They point out that perhaps the biggest handicap is in the fact "that the popular conception of the successful leader in America is someone who himself can assess situations rapidly and successfully and

---

[4] George Sharp, *Curriculum Development As Re-education of the Teacher* (New York: Teachers College, Bureau of Publications, Columbia University, 1951), p. 86.

[5] Laura Zirbes, *Focus on Values in Elementary Education* (New York: G. P. Putnam's Sons, 1960), No. 1.

can get other people to do whatever he thinks needs to be done." [6]

Proponents of democratic administration must realize that the administrative role is not an easy one. As indicated above, tradition has given the public and the staff an image that is deeply embedded in popular thinking. The administrator has his own image of his role. The school board to which he is responsible has an image of him which, in many cases, is not democratic in operation. School programs have become so extremely complex and so demanding that, whether right or not, the administrator often lacks the time to devote to playing the role in a genuinely democratic fashion. Each day he is confronted with problems that require quick decisions. These problems often cannot wait to be resolved by a meeting of the minds of the faculty members. But perhaps even more challenging than all of this is the task of acquiring the technical and the sensitive ability to work with diverse groups encountering a wide array of problems. Some years ago, Kenneth Benne appropriately said: "Democratic leadership requires attitudes, understandings, and skills which are more, not less, profound and complex than those required by the autocratic leader." [7]

Any number of thoughtful people, lay or professional, will bring to the group their individual antagonisms, stereotype concepts, and everyday preferences and prejudices. The problems these psychological barriers present are commonly more numerous when the schools work with lay people. One can be reasonably certain that the larger the cross section of the community represented, the greater will be the diversity of opinions as to school needs. The administrator, however, needs to have confidence in the possible training of these diverse individuals to accept some common goals. The school is an ongoing actuality. It is a fact that it has a purpose in a democracy. It is a fact that people have already learned to cooperate to some degree.

Some specific problems that challenge the administration and tend to retard growth and progress are the following:

1. The participants fail to have a clear concept of what they hope to achieve;

---

[6] American Association of School Administrators, *The Superintendent As Instructional Leader, op. cit.,* p. 40.

[7] Kenneth Benne, "Leaders Are Made, Not Born," *Childhood Education,* Vol. XXIV (January, 1948), 203.

2. Some may regard the amount of time required to get an in-service program underway as an unnecessary loss of time;
3. The "loss of time" problem *may* become more serious if a faculty has not had former experience in working as a group or if adequate assistance from a consultant is lacking;
4. In contrast, some groups are so highly structured that individual initiative and creativity are seriously curtailed;
5. Personality problems or administrative directives may obstruct communication;
6. The process of change may lack an acceptable method of evaluation;
7. There may be one or more impulsive persons who have a hobby-horse or otherwise must speak or act excessively;
8. Some subgroups of a faculty or a school system may fail to use the best informed people;
9. The group may proceed in such a manner that there is no orderly arrangement of progress or achievement and therefore no plan to use;
10. Some groups may become so concerned with trivia that they do not require any depth of thinking or of learning;
11. Teacher groups may feel dissatisfaction because the entire program constitutes an extra duty;
12. Participants may sense failure because there is no attempt to apply a change of behavior to actual teaching programs;
13. The group may be too large for wide participation.

Wilbur A. Yauch suggests that the faculty is the best working group "interacting with other organic wholes, to make up the administrative unit of the school system." [8]

The Administrator as a Participant

If the administrator's role is most complex, this only adds to the claim that he has the greatest need for in-service education. Some reasons that justify this assertion are:

1. Modern educational programs are complex and this trend appears to be destined to continue;
2. The impact of change demands new thinking and behavior;
3. Destructive forces and criticisms of public education have become so extensive that new insights and interpretations must be developed;
4. The administrator can no longer "go it alone": he desperately needs the knowledge that is available within the staff;

---

[8] Wilbur A. Yauch, *Improving Human Relations in School Administration* (New York: Harper & Row, Publishers, 1949), pp. 13–14.

5. Research must be continuous and must be made available to him by others;

6. He must play a major role in human relations, both within the school or school system and with the public.

The Administration and the Beginning Teacher

Each year thousands of young college graduates enter the teaching profession. They meet new people—many of which are teachers who have taught in the same situation for years and consequently have made some adjustments and are free from a feeling of strangeness. This awareness of others' adjustments adds to the concerns of the beginner. The new teacher is sensitive to the differences in experience. Not only are the people new, but the very anticipation of the act of teaching is frightening. Teachers, students, books, the curriculum—everything is new. In many—perhaps in most—cases, it is the beginning teacher's first major responsibility in a position in which both money and the welfare of other people are at stake.

One other thing that beginning teachers have in common: they all want to succeed—failure is a horrifying prospect. To whom do they go for help? Probably the help most needed is psychological: the acceptance, understanding, and support of the professional staff —particularly the administration.

The extent to which new teachers will accept an in-service education program depends substantially upon the degree to which it is or has been accepted by experienced teachers within the school or school system. E. Paul Torrance [9] has shown that inexperienced people are readily influenced by those with more experience, unless to some the experience has been an unhappy one. However, it is also known that teachers who have transferred from another school system are often reluctant to accept new procedures if former experiences were satisfying to them.

Many observers have recognized the problems encountered by beginning teachers, and during recent years many methods of limiting this continuing weakness of education in this country have been suggested. It has been pointed out by Strickler that "the first year of teaching is a process of continuous adjustment, extending over the

---

[9] E. Paul Torrance, "The Influence of Experienced Members of Small Groups on the Behavior of the Inexperienced," *Journal of Social Psychology*, Vol. 49 (1959), 249–57.

entire year and constituting a series of problems, both professional and personal in nature." [10]

Although most young teachers enter their first teaching assignment filled with anticipation of new adventure and determined to succeed in a professional capacity, they too often become disheartened and discouraged because their zest for the new and the untried is thwarted by the administration. For most of these teachers, Frederick Mayer says, "teaching has ceased to be an adventure and instead has become drudgery." [11]

Administrative Details of Major Importance

As indicated above, the administrator is largely responsible for establishing the emotional climate within which the school operates. He may or may not originate the in-service education program, but he is inescapably a facilitator of it once it is underway; and in this capacity he becomes one who shares, supports, and encourages. But there are details for which he is responsible and must have the cooperation of his colleagues. For example, there are those many reports that appear to characterize all school systems. Teachers tend to ask: "Why are these important?" "When must they be completed?" "How can I do this and teach?" All these questions and more will be asked unless there is understanding. With understanding usually comes acceptance. Certainly, teachers need to be convinced of the importance of reports (and other requirements), and this conviction can come only with insight as to purpose.

The calling of a faculty meeting to obtain a consensus or a majority vote of every little detail is absurd and indicates administrative weakness. Meetings take valuable teacher time and should be held only on regularly approved schedule or in case of a problem of major importance. However, the administrator of a school or a school system is endlessly confronted with problems requiring decisions and it is important that the school arrive at a consensus as to the kinds of decisions he will make alone, in consultation with a committee or with the entire faculty.

---

[10] Robert W. Strickler, "Follow Through with the First-Year Teacher," *Educational Administration and Supervision*, Vol. 45 (January, 1959), 1–2.

[11] Frederick Mayer, "Educating for Creativity," *Phi Delta Kappan*, Vol. XXXV, No. 5 (February, 1954), 195.

Developing a Philosophy
within the School System

Every school system intentionally or unconsciously develops its own particular philosophy. This may be explicitly stated, or it may be implied in the feelings, attitudes toward change and growth, and relationships among school personnel. Whether implicit or explicit, it is real.

The modern philosophy of an individual school or a school system is based upon democratic principles, and these become much of the foundation on which the in-service education program rests. Some of these principles are the following:

1. An honest recognition of the integrity and worth of each person who is a part of the school system;
2. A willingness to share responsibility and information;
3. A desire for self- and school improvement;
4. Horizontal rather than vertical channels of communication;
5. A willingness to admit error with a desire to learn to be right;
6. An atmosphere of freedom to learn and to teach.

Planning the In-Service Education Program

In-service education programs are of many kinds, but here we will emphasize that in which a school system, a faculty, a segment of the faculty (such as teachers of a given grade or given subject in one or more schools) who may have a common interest come together for the purpose of learning and making changes in an ongoing program.

Without appearing to be an organizing genius, the administrator may offer suggestions as to patterns of organization in which the study program may be most effective. He may help (but only help) identify problems of interest. However, social scientists have repeatedly asserted that the success of in-service programs largely depends upon the degree to which teachers themselves identify their problems. The recognition of one's inability or of the need for change in order to grow, dissatisfaction with one's behavior in teaching, or a determined effort to improve the school or the school system are more successful in motivating productive teacher action than are orders to do or not to do.

The administrator may well serve in the capacity of coordinating in-service education if such programs extend to more than one group. He may, if the group feels the need, provide for consulting help from outside the school district.

In summary, it may be said that the administrator has both unique and specific duties because of his status position, but he, with others, must grow as a part of the in-service education program. As one of the group he may help to select the area for study, to plan the pattern of personnel organization, to design the method of research and investigation, and to evaluate both the process of growth and any other achievement of concern to the group. Perhaps most important, he needs to forget his status position and be a model of democratic procedure.

Action Programs with Teacher Cooperation

There is substantial evidence that teachers become highly motivated in seeking solutions to school problems that, at the moment of action, may be remote from their immediate teaching. Education has to its credit some important achievements as a result of teachers' involvement in such problems as improvement of school legislation, consolidation of small schools, and reorganization of school districts. Teachers are capable of studying problems of school finance; during recent years they have contributed greatly to school building planning. The challenge to the administrator is to furnish the leadership under which an atmosphere conducive to growth may be one that is readily acceptable to teachers. This atmosphere of growth from experimentation and for change must largely be the result of the administrator's working philosophy. This is particularly true if the problems on which teachers are to work are not those that challenge them at the moment or in the classroom.

A case in point may be the creation of an atmosphere in which teachers may provide productive help in school building planning. For many years school buildings, and particularly classrooms within a given building, were essentially alike. Recent changes in which school faculties have participated may be observed in the annual exhibit of school building designs sponsored by the American Association of School Administrators. These plans differ substantially from those of school buildings of earlier years. One major reason for the difference is that teachers have participated in the planning. Their imagination and creativity have been encouraged to find expression in these plans. Increasingly, these building plans are designed to house the best educational program teachers can conceive.

The Related Role of the Teacher in In-Service Education

Only under those circumstances in which teachers find their own problems and want to do something about them can effective in-service education programs exist. Freedom to grow as one chooses must not be interpreted as license to do nothing. The better school systems develop a contagious attitude which assumes that the professional person has a duty and a desire to improve. Even the unchanging person seems to get in the circle of interest and tends to become dissatisfied with his work in such an atmosphere of change and progress.

Some teachers may need assistance in discovering their own problems. They, therefore, need to help in establishing some criteria by which they can evaluate their own teaching. The faculty of an entire school system should actively participate in revising the philosophy of the school and the objectives of education. If teachers do not know the objectives of the school, they will not know where they are going or how to get there. If they do, they have a definite commitment to work for the goals which they help to establish. Objectives toward which they are working under such circumstances become *their* goals, and they feel possessive toward them.

There are conditions of mutual responsibility under which in-service growth will likely be effective. Among these are the following:

1. An awareness on the part of the professional staff that educational growth is needed;

2. A willingness to devote the necessary time and energy involved in study as a means of in-service education;

3. The support and cooperation of the board of education;

4. A corps of highly professional and progressive school administrators;

5. A school district policy that places value on experimentation, creative effort, and innovations in the school;

6. A school policy that can provide the necessary time for research and group study.

Although this chapter emphasizes the role of the administration in facilitating in-service education programs, it must be noted that administration does not exist in a vacuum: it exists in relation to other people and what they do. It is necessary, therefore, to note the mutuality of in-service education. In order for the teacher to grow successfully, he must possess certain qualities. Among these are the following:

1. The desire to grow;
2. The readiness to participate;
3. A sensitivity to the opinions of others;
4. Intelligence and knowledgeability;
5. A willingness to discard unproductive habits of teaching;
6. The desire to accept new challenges even though they require added effort and present some uncertainty.

Teachers need to be future-oriented, to have a certain discontent with the present and to understand that hard work will be encountered in the days to come because growth is a process without end. They need to know they don't have to be like other good teachers. The teacher needs to recognize that he is a learner and that everything he learns changes him so that he is continuously becoming a different person.

He learns as he makes decisions and choices. The thrill and excitement of learning within the group come because the processes of exchanging ideas and building new concepts add to his power to be selective and enable him to choose what he wants to make a part of himself. It is this experiencing and growth that enlarges the powers of judgment to make new choices. The greater the fluency and frequency of ideas of the group in analyzing a problem, the more selective the learner can be in choosing what he will add to himself.

Deciding Whom to Include

The very large school systems are composed of too many people to work effectively as a single group. Divisions need to be made and a coordinating committee must be established to bring together the ideas of all participants. In smaller systems professionals may find it better to work together on certain problems involving teacher growth and understanding. This is particularly so when they select for study an area involving personnel problems, methods of evaluating progress of a school system, revisions of the objectives of education, or recommendations of policies for analysis by the school board.

The best unit of organization of in-service education for most problems appears to be the individual school faculty. There are reasons why this is so. The members are more likely to have a common interest. Dissimilar interests occur when faculties of different age groups meet. The problems kindergarten teachers face in helping five-year-olds adjust to their first social experiences away from home would not challenge the interest of the science teachers in the senior high school. Teachers within a given school soon become acquainted, thereby removing the barrier of strangeness that would be present if they were from different schools. The single faculty study group finds it much more convenient to remain at its own building and thereby saves the time and expense of traveling to other school buildings.

The size of the group is an important factor. In a large group only a few members have an opportunity to express their ideas. This is not the best way to cultivate growth. Growth comes as the individual reacts to an idea conveyed by another—particularly if the reaction is expressed, for then the person extends himself. The importance of the interplay of ideas can hardly be overemphasized. A faculty may meet to arrive at a consensus on the over-all problems to be studied and thereafter divide into smaller groups. These smaller groups need to meet to analyze and work at problems of interest to them. The size of the group may be two or more. The determining factor should be of common interest in a given problem. "Contact" persons among the groups may be appointed.

Likewise, it may be noted that the length of time involved for any of these groups may vary from a few minutes to a year or longer. Usually, the larger groups become involved in problems requiring more time.

The participation of people from outside the professional staff likewise depends on the nature of the problem. Consultants may appropriately participate if the group sees the need for special help, if the problem or problems are of such magnitude that a contribution can be made by a consultant, and if consultant help is available and can be secured by the school system.

It has become popular, particularly since World War II, to invite community groups to participate with the professionals in study programs. It is maintained by many that this is an excellent method of strengthening public relations. Although good public relations may be necessary for the protection and advancement of the public schools, it is doubtful that such participation is necessary or desirable under all circumstances. It likely would be necessary if the staff had tentatively arrived at a belief that the school district should erect more school buildings and for this purpose a bonding program was necessary. It may be desirable to invite patrons to help decide the best way of communicating the progress of students to parents. There is some doubt as to the wisdom of lay participation on other problems that are distinctly professional. Laymen can make little or no contribution, for instance, in the selection of teachers. They may or may not be able to help the administration in the allocation of anticipated expenditures in certain items of the school budget. In other words, many variables enter into the administration of the schools, and the particular problem must be isolated and analyzed before one can say with certainty who shall be included in the study program.

Evaluating the Results of In-Service Education

The school administration has the responsibility of helping to establish an acceptable method of evaluating major programs of in-service education. Without such methods, there are no valid ways of evaluating changes within the school or measuring growth on the part of the faculty. The evaluation instruments, like all other segments of in-service education involving the faculty of one or more schools, must emerge as a cooperative effort. In fact, developing the answers to the following three questions of evaluation is an excellent in-service educational device:

1. What are the characteristics and qualities of the *best* school the group can describe?

2. What are the areas of strength and of weakness in the school in which the group teaches?

3. What needs to be done in order to move the qualities of the school in which teachers have concern to those qualities of the best school perceived?

Each school district, each school, and each teacher should have carefully analyzed objectives. Without such objectives, change and progress cannot be determined. These objectives must change as progress is made. As the objectives change, the teacher is challenged to change his behavior. It is possible that, as the teacher learns, the gap between his behavior and the goals he seeks will widen.

CHAPTER VI

In-Service Education
Through Democratic Processes

Teachers bring their past with them as they enter the teaching profession. Many, perhaps most, come from highly regulated families and autocratically controlled schools. They have been taught that the schools are to educate children in such a way that democracy will be preserved, freedom extended, and the rights of the individual enlarged. But when they face a group as teachers, their insecurity and fear of failure prevent behavior that complies with the democratic ideals. Under these circumstances, differences in the ways individual teachers relate to others soon begin to appear. The insecure teacher develops behavior that neither enhances his own growth or extends that of the students toward modern objectives. In contrast, the teacher who has learned and lived freedom and who has extended himself in that environment continues to grow as do the students who learn and live with him.

The prospective teacher must learn to understand the peculiar role of the school. Other professions, such as medicine or law, provide services that are personal and temporary. Differing from these, the schools, while providing a service to individuals, are essentially social. They have the mission of creating an environment for growth in which each person extends himself toward both an immediate and a future goal. In addition to developing the individual, the school has the great responsibility of providing the kind of education that will guarantee the perpetuation and expansion of democracy.

It is this great responsibility of teachers that makes an in-service education program imperative. Teachers have not received before entering the teaching profession—nor could they have received— all the education they need to enable them to widen and deepen the principles of democracy, both in their own lives and the lives of their students. In other words, in-service education in democratic living with students becomes a necessary part of teaching.

If the effective teacher is adequately to assist children to learn and live democracy, he himself must learn the complex social skills needed for this purpose. More than a score of years ago, Bode declared that students do not learn the ways of democracy outside the school. He stated they bring to school beliefs and attitudes that "do not fit acceptably into the philosophy that is adopted and practiced by a democratic school." [1]

He further declared:

> The school must undertake to exemplify . . . its conception of democratic living. This is necessary, not merely to promote a better intellectual understanding of democracy, but to create the conditions for transforming democratic precepts into established habits of feeling and willing. In brief, the school must be a place where pupils go, not merely to learn, but to carry on a way of life. [2]

The importance of teachers working and learning in an atmosphere free from authoritarian control is emphasized in the 1962 Yearbook of the Association for Supervision and Curriculum Development. [3] The point of view expressed therein is that one cannot be a fully functioning person in an authoritarian culture in which he acts out of fear and frustration and is deprived of being involved in problem situations. It is through cooperative effort that one learns to be a "fully functioning self" and develops human values by understanding others. He profits by mistakes without harm to his personality because he is sensitive to a moving flow of experience. He accepts "self" without becoming "selfish."

An effective program of in-service education that is based upon the optimal growth of all professionals concerned and the utilization of democratic processes for growth does not preclude numerous decisions that must be made by the individual. Teaching is not a single process but a combination of many complex interactions that change moment by moment. No one interaction is ever exactly like the preceding one, or will it be like the one that follows. Each in-

---

[1] Boyd H. Bode, *Democracy As A Way of Life* (New York: The Macmillan Company, 1939), p. 85.

[2] *Ibid.*, p. 77.

[3] Association for Supervision and Curriculum Development, *Perceiving, Behaving, Becoming: A New Focus for Education* 1962 Yearbook (Washington, D.C.: National Education Association, 1962).

cident calls for decision-making at the time of its occurrence. Decisions are more likely to be correct if they are based upon the shared experiences of the teachers and the students.

Indecision does not characterize the successful teacher. Indecision leads to frustration, uncertainty, and—ultimately—chaos. Learning to make wise decisions by working with a group is basic to quality education. The process of making such decisions is one that must grow with experience that is shared. The immature teacher, the teacher who does not have confidence in others, will tend to revert to autocratic behavior unless he can find democratic values in other people. This gulf of differences in behavior is wide. Kurt Lewin said:

> Autocracy is imposed upon the individual; democracy, he has to learn. . . .
>
> Learning democracy means, firstly, that the person has to do something himself instead of being passively moved by forces imposed on him. Secondly, learning democracy means to establish certain likes and dislikes, that is, certain valences, values, and ideologies. Thirdly, learning democracy means to get acquainted with certain techniques, for instance, those of group decision.[4]

Learning the Nature of the Group

A group can more easily be described than defined. An assembly of individuals is not necessarily a group. Those who are members of a group are aware of such membership. They are held together by a common interest. The members establish loyalties to the objectives of the group and become aware of group pressure if their behavior departs from that prescribed. The group has expectations of each person, and of itself that motivate patterns of action. Without such expectations the group becomes nonproductive and tends to deteriorate.

The fact that great numbers of school people spend much time in groups of different sizes as they work toward the solution of problems is not necessarily an indication that the group process is always productive of success. In fact, it may be a frustrating and psycho-

---

[4] Kurt Lewin, *The Psychology of Learning,* in Yearbook of the National Society for the Study of Education, Part II, Nelson B. Henry, ed. (Bloomington, Ill.: Public School Publishing Co., 1942), p. 231.

logically damaging experience. Matthew B. Miles has clearly stated that working in groups is a skill that must be learned if the process is to be on a high level.[5]

The existence of a group gives no assurance that growth will automatically result. Only those groups that can agree on common goals are likely to extend themselves toward these goals.

Max R. Goodson says: "The critical question is whether the group reinforces a person in a desirable direction or restrains him from desirable behavior." [6]

The effectiveness of a group as a means of in-service education of teachers is largely determined by the ability of the group members to free themselves from individual tensions and anxieties. This ability is not possessed by all people. Differences in academic education, former experience in comparable situations, previous successes or failures in one's work, and administrative procedures all have an important role to play. The person who dares not trust himself or others suffers serious handicaps, and he is limited in an interchange of ideas with others.

Past experiences may obstruct or enhance the flow of ideas, depending upon the quality of such experiences. Some people find approbation and a feeling of power in situations in which they can work with others on an interpersonal basis, suggests Timothy Leary.[7] Such people may or may not contribute effectively to the group. A possible danger is that the satisfaction derived from being heard may give rise to excessive talking rather than an effective sharing of knowledge.

The group may establish its own procedural criteria and determine its methods of growth as a result of research in the behavioral sciences. In-service education is the only force that can keep interpersonal competence current. Nelson N. Foote and Leonard S. Cottrell, Jr., have said this "interpersonal competence . . . denotes ca-

---

[5] Matthew B. Miles, *Learning to Work in Groups* (New York: Teachers College, Bureau of Publications, Columbia University, 1959), pp. 1–2.

[6] Max R. Goodson, "The 'Person' and the 'Group' in American Education," in *The Dynamics of Instructional Groups,* The Fifty-Ninth Yearbook of the National Society for the Study of Education, Part II, Nelson B. Henry, ed. (Chicago: University of Chicago Press, 1960), p. 15.

[7] Timothy Leary, *Interpersonal Diagnosis of Personality* (New York: The Ronald Press Company, 1957), pp. 323-24.

pabilities to meet and deal with a changing world, to formulate ends and implement them.[8]

Growth is most likely to take place in a teacher group in which interpersonal relations are such that all persons participate and move toward an acceptable goal—a goal that can be moved forward as learning takes place. In such a group each person should be free from antagonism toward others or toward the purpose serving to motivate the group. Growth likewise is best when the unpredictable person or situation is regarded, not as an undesirable phenomenon but as a possible means of acquiring a new insight or meeting new needs. Pritzkau states: "It is somewhat depressing to find that, in some groups, the majority of individuals behave in such a predictable manner that any deviation regardless of quality may be met with rejection." [9]

Not only are school faculties confronted with a great variety of problems but circumstances emerge that do much to determine the climate in which teachers will work toward their solution. Too often teachers assemble hastily to solve problems with which they are unacquainted or that appear to be urgent. A number of studies have been made to determine the degree of integration or disintegration that attends a crisis. If the crisis situation is accepted by the group as having a possible solution, the motivation and integration of the group are increased. But if a solution cannot be found, the group tends to disintegrate and to become ineffective.[10]

Teacher groups are commonly heterogeneous in terms of maturity and are not equally effective in attaining a given goal. Some problems are not challenging to all teachers. Others may be so abstract or obscure that some or all members of the group may not be motivated toward an established goal. More intelligent or more experienced persons work better when confronted with challenges of greater depth. In such cases it appears necessary for the participants to be able to explore and create their own innovations toward possible solutions.

---

[8] Nelson N. Foote and Leonard S. Cottrell, Jr., *Identity and Interpersonal Competence* (Chicago: University of Chicago Press, 1955), p. 49.

[9] Philo T. Pritzkau, *Dynamics of Curriculum Development* (Englewood Cliffs, N.J.: Prentice-Hall, Inc., 1959), p. 380.

[10] Robert L. Hamblin, "Group Integration During a Crisis," *Human Relations*, Vol. XI, No. 1 (1958), 67–76.

Another very real danger may exist when all the members of the group come from the middle class of society. In such cases, their values, their education, their anxieties, and their aspirations may be so similar that they will be cheated of the challenges provided by differences in these areas. Such challenges are not known unless their study contacts extend to individuals from upper or lower classes as well as from conservative and liberal groups on the same general social level.

Ideally, each member of a study group must willingly accept responsibility to share his own problems and his information with others. Everyone loses when some member of the group fails to contribute. The group thrives upon ideas and ideas seem to multiply as they are shared among the participants. As indicated above, some teachers find it difficult to work in teams or groups. Only people who can be comfortable when their own preferences and prejudices are known to others can work well in a group. Many have had long experience with the belief that the possession of deep-seated prejudices is an indication of strong character. The learning process itself, in which a given body of "preferred" subject matter or a "preferred" method of teaching is stressed, may handicap a teacher.

The group will be able to accomplish more if the nature of its working together is such that anxieties and threats to individual status will be held to a minimum. However, limited anxiety on the part of one member or of a group may serve as a motivating force in the search for new ideas, providing the anxiety is an impelling rather than a restraining force. Threats to status will tend to be overcome to the degree that mutuality exists. According to Philo T. Pritzkau,[11] in order to develop this mutuality it is necessary for each of the participants to analyze his own feelings, aspirations, and sense of values and—in the process—to be sufficiently submissive in the ongoing program to find satisfaction in receiving support and supporting others while working toward an acceptance of a common goal.

In-Service Education: A Cooperative Endeavor

Public schools are natural social instruments for cooperative learning and afford an excellent laboratory for the growth of people

---

[11] Pritzkau, *op. cit.*, p. 378.

on a large scale. One such example may be noted in a comprehensive high school. Properly conceived as a device for in-service education, the larger or more comprehensive the school offering, the greater will be the opportunity of pooling the background and information of an enlarged number of teachers representing different disciplines. Donald C. Manlove has pointed this out: "Here are professionally trained people representing different disciplines, vitally interested in the education of boys and girls, and ready to contribute time and energy to curriculum study." [12]

The importance of the group process in in-service teacher education is recommended universally by authors who have studied this problem. Numerous experiments have provided evidence that individuals do not think at the highest level of their potential when and if they think alone. Both depth and breadth of thinking are increased as a result of the interaction with others. The responses, spoken or not, the individual makes to the ideas of others are the stuff of which growth is made. Lane and Beauchamp described this when they said: "Each person screens his perception by his own responses." [13] These responses have a dual value: they create growth in the person who "screens his perception" in a response, and they cause others to screen their own perceptions as the interactive process proceeds.

The individual's ability to learn only a fraction of the facts as they are accumulating is an impelling reason for the exchanging and sharing of knowledge. Much of what one attempts to learn alone is not actually learned well. The group is able to do much not only to add to one's knowledge but to clarify it and make it more usable. It is not unusual to find a classroom teacher whose performance is based upon erroneous concepts. The group often can prevent or correct such a performance when it becomes observable to the group or to the person concerned from an analysis by others. Group decisions are more likely to be valid and verifiable. Experimental evidence clearly indicates that the individual develops clearer and more usable concepts by group participation than would be the case if he were building concepts limited to his own experience.

---

[12] Donald C. Manlove, "Organizing the Faculty for Curriculum Improvement," *Bulletin of the National Association of Secondary-School Principals,* Vol. 43, No. 244 (February, 1959), 57.

[13] Howard Lane and Mary Beauchamp, *Human Relations in Teaching* (Englewood Cliffs, N.J.: Prentice-Hall, Inc., 1955), p. 58.

Phillip M. Marcus has verified such studies as those of the Survey Research Center at Ann Arbor, Michigan, indicating that increased production and higher morale exist where there is group orientation.[14]

Among the reasons that faculty members should work as a group for growth are the following:

1. They can more readily and more accurately identify or limit a problem of common concern;
2. They are more selective in establishing a method of searching for answers;
3. They are able to analyze divergent points of view on any problem;
4. They can objectively evaluate an ongoing program;
5. They are able to analyze objectively the process of their group growth;
6. They can alter or expand their program of investigation;
7. They can share information;
8. They develop group interest and understanding;
9. They locate personal problems thwarting progress;
10. They are able to arrive at conclusions that change behavior;
11. They can implement decisions as they are made, thereby changing individual and group behavior.

The nature of growth in an individual who is a participant in a group is different from that in one who works alone. The individual comes to build an attachment to the process of group action. He can more clearly perceive change and growth because of an awareness of the meshing of his ideas with those of others. Kimball Wiles has said of the group process: "Loyalty ceases to be loyalty to persons; it becomes loyalty to ideas." [15]

Dynamics of the Group

Perhaps nothing better characterizes the quality of the modern school program than the degree to which the faculty within a given school or the total professional staff of a school system learn and work together. For a quarter of a century or more, scholars in the behavioral sciences have been experimenting and observing the

---

[14] Phillip M. Marcus, "Supervision of Group Process," *Human Organization,* Vol. 20, No. 1 (Spring, 1961), 15–19.

[15] Kimball Wiles, "Where Does Cooperation Start?" *Educational Leadership,* Vol. XI, No. 5 (February, 1954), 309.

problems, processes, and productions of people working within a group. Certain individual differences may retard effective group growth and effective production, but some differences are needful. In recent years many schools (some as part of a research program to determine the effectiveness of group work) have launched various programs of in-service education utilizing group study and group research as a means of adding quality to the curriculum and adding professional stature to the staff.

In a school or a school system in which an ongoing program of in-service education has been successful and in which a majority of mature teachers have had the benefits of belonging to a group, the initiation of a study-growth program is easier. As Harold G. Shane and Wilbur A. Yauch have said: "A sense of belonging is a powerful force in bringing satisfaction to the teacher. All human beings wish to feel that they belong; that they are important to the welfare and the success of the group." [16]

Not only do the members of a group acquire added information and develop new patterns of teaching from these experiences, but the morale of the staff is usually greatly heightened as a result of this process.

The morale of a group is increased when (a) the individual is recognized for his contributions to the group, (b) when he is given responsibility for the development of better ways of enhancing the school program, and (c) when responsibility is shared among several persons rather than lodged in a single person.

Interaction and Learning

Much has been learned during this century about the nature of learning from experimentation. We now know that effective learning does not take place in situations that fail to provide the learner with certain responses and reactions. The traditional schools failed to produce high levels of learning for a number of reasons, but primarily because they gave no consideration to the individual's readiness to learn. Learning does not take place because one is ordered to learn. One learns little or nothing unless he understands the pur-

---

[16] Harold G. Shane and Wilbur A. Yauch, *Creative School Administration* (New York: Holt, Rinehart and Winston, Inc., 1954), p. 105.

pose or need for learning. On the other hand, one learns best when he accepts the goals for learning and has shared in establishing the goals. Learning is a process that requires insight into purpose and a feeling of satisfaction as it matures. It is reacting toward one's environment and receiving motivation from the environment to extend oneself toward newer experiences. Since people are most important in one's environment, learning is relating to and reacting toward others. Learning, then, is a process of interaction. For the child at school, learning is determined by the way he acts and reacts to the teachers and others as they act and react toward him. According to Howard Lane and Mary Beauchamp: "Most of human learning does not result from deliberate conscious instruction but rather from the interrelationships of human beings as they develop in social situations." [17]

Teachers learn as children do. They do not learn by receiving mandates from others. They, too, learn most effectively in a group of their colleagues when they recognize needs and are motivated with others to solve problems. Teacher learning, like child learning, is a process of interaction. The amount or quality of interaction can be determined by such factors as group morale, understanding and acceptance of the purpose for which the group is established, the individual's willingness to share his best with others, the skill each person—and therefore the group—possesses with original or creative ideas, the clarification of one's perceptions as the process moves toward the goals, the amount of change as the process continues to extend, and the desire for and ability to make application of concluding recommendations.

Encouraging Creativity as a Means of Professional Growth

Only creative, imaginative teachers can make a climate for growth that gives encouragement to creative students. The school that centers in-service education for teachers about such topics as "courses of study," "textbooks," "reports," and "discipline" does an injustice to teachers. The teacher who expresses pride in students' mastery of subject matter, an orderly classroom, and above-standard

---

[17] Lane and Beauchamp, *op. cit.,* p. 70.

norm rankings on academic subject matter tests for which he "drilled" the students will not encourage creative potential in the young.

Uniformity and independent growth cannot exist in the same classroom. John L. Holland has reported on a study: "The results suggest that creative performance at the high school level occurs more frequently among students who are independent, intellectual, expressive, asocial, consciously original, and who have high aspirations for future achievement." [18]

These students manifested behavior that was quite different from that of the academic achievers in the same study.

One of the tragedies met by creative people (students and teachers) is that they often become social outcasts. In fact, Robert H. Beck found that such children were "unwanted by both their peers and their teachers." [19]

People (including some administrators and fellow teachers) who are disturbed when the normal and established methods or rules are questioned are not comfortable with creative people. Parents become irritated because creative children question the family values. These children do this because it is the normal thing for them to extend themselves into new ways of doing. They want to live an open life and without hesitation or embarrassment violate the norms as they project themselves into the unusual.

Unless teachers have the proper education and understanding, they will find this behavior challenging. However, the line of demarcation between the creative and noncreative person is not necessarily clear in most cases. People who are free to experiment or to explore appear to expand this ability. Earl C. Kelley and Marie I. Rasey believe the "great volume of creativity" is in those people who do "contrive." They claim: "Unique contriving is the flower of the thinking process. It can bloom only in a climate of freedom. It is the growing edge of discovery and invention, the method of progress." [20]

---

[18] John L. Holland, "Creative and Academic Performance Among Talented Adolescents," *Journal of Educational Psychology*, Vol. 52, No. 3 (1961), 146.

[19] Robert H. Beck, "Society and Individual Differences," *Individualizing Instruction*, The Sixty-First Yearbook of the National Society for the Study of Education, Part I, Nelson B. Henry, ed. (Chicago: University of Chicago Press, 1962), p. 28.

[20] Earl C. Kelley and Marie I. Rasey, *Education and the Nature of Man* (New York: Harper & Row, Publishers, 1952), p. 116.

Schools making promising progress have creativity at both the teaching and student level. Students cannot develop creative tendencies without freedom to make innovations. When all answers must be the answers expected by the book, creativity will not thrive. Machine teaching that offers no exceptions to the "correct" answer will not permit creative growth. The creative teacher is one who views an old problem or situation from a new or altered perspective. The teacher and the student must work together, not so much to find answers as to devise "problem" approaches with innovations. Nelson N. Foote and Leonard S. Cottrell, Jr., describe this interpersonal relation as "the ability to invent or improve new roles or alternative lines of action in problematic situations, and to evoke such behavior in others. Among other things, it seems to involve curiosity, self-confidence, something of the venturesome and risk-taking tendencies of the explorer." [21]

Lindley J. Stiles has appropriately said: "It is ironic that, at a time when teaching needs most to be strengthened, a nationwide campaign is being conducted to support the premise that scholarship in a subject field alone is sufficient to successful teaching." [22]

Similarly, Ernest O. Melby and Floyd W. Reeves have declared:

> More than ever the school must become the one place in the life of the individual . . . where people can differ with safety, where originality can be encouraged. . . . To have such schools, we must have teachers who have not succumbed to the comformist mood, who are still seeking the truth, who are more fearful of untruth and of unsound action than of nonconformity.[23]

In summary, one may say that if this nation is to progress and change for the better as it has been doing in the past, the schools must play a major role. Teachers are under pressure to conform. The administration, also under pressure, is looking for systems and for crosscuts. New developments, such as teaching machines and commercially prepared programs for learning, now widely publi-

---

[21] Nelson N. Foote and Leonard S. Cottrell, Jr., *Identity and Interpersonal Relations* (Chicago: University of Chicago Press, 1955), p. 57.

[22] Lindley J. Stiles, "Creative Teaching for Excellence in Education," *School and Society* (September, 1955), 355.

[23] Ernest O. Melby and Floyd W. Reeves, "Education and the Evolving Nature of Society," in *Personnel Services in Education,* The Fifty-Eighth Yearbook of the National Society for the Study of Education, Part II, Nelson B. Henry, ed. (Chicago: University of Chicago Press, 1959), p. 23.

cized, all have an impact on education. The great challenge is not to conform but to encourage climates of growth in which teachers may be different and seek the unusual without fear or intimidation. Teacher behavior with students must not be imitative but fresh and freedom-giving as it explores the challenging and the unknown. The quality of in-service education will largely determine the quality of teaching. Progress and improvement will come if the schools are not typed but helped to be unique.

Leadership and In-Service Education

A relatively new concept is that leadership in a democracy appropriately shifts from person to person as one after another contributes ideas that extend or push the group effort in the direction of the goal that is sought. From this point of view leadership may be best described, not as a position of status or the permanent posession of one person, but as a sharing of the role depending upon the person or persons who possess the most valuable information leading to the solution of a given problem. Leadership, under this definition, is group-centered and may shift freely from person to person and situation to situation. It is a process of interaction. According to Thomas Gordon: "Leadership stands for a particular kind of interpersonal relationship between human beings." [24]

An abundance of evidence now exists that leadership lodged in one or more status leaders cannot meet the needs of teachers and students in a school system when democracy is to be learned and lived and a rapidly expanding body of knowledge must continue to grow.

Other scholars take a point of view similar to that of Gordon. Herbert A. Thelen says: "Leadership is the set of functions through which the group coordinates the efforts of individuals." [25]

The 1960 Yearbook of the Association for Supervision and Curriculum Development defines educational leadership as *that action or behavior among individuals and groups which causes both the*

---

[24] Thomas Gordon, *Group-Centered Leadership* (Boston: Houghton Mifflin Company, 1955), p. 23.

[25] Herbert A. Thelen, *Dynamics of Groups at Work* (Chicago: University of Chicago Press, 1943), p. 297.

*individual and the groups to move toward educational goals that are
increasingly mutually acceptable to them."* [26]

Matthew B. Miles has analyzed several aspects of leadership as
a part of "learning to work in groups" and asserts: "A functional
view of leadership . . . is [that] this view tends to lead to the belief
that leadership is learnable, and is shared by many group members,
instead of being only a matter of one person's behavior." [27]

Margaret E. Bennett maintains, "One of the most challenging
aspects of in-service training within an educational setting is the
fact that it can draw upon all of the firsthand experiences of trainees
in a living laboratory. . . ." [28]

David H. Jenkins lists seven items believed to be necessary for
the development of effective leadership. The seventh states effective
leadership can be developed by the teacher if "he [the teacher] is
willing to be influenced by the students in the same manner he ex-
pects them to be influenced by him." [29]

For decades the school executive has been in the role of the "front
man." He has received the criticism or the praise for the quality of
the schools. This role has not always been an easy one. His tenure
(particularly in the case of the superintendent) has usually been
brief. The issues and problems facing him have been many, forcing
him to be a decision-maker whether or not he would so choose. He
now must make another choice in his role of leadership: Will it be
leader-centered or group-centered? If he sees his role as one of attempting to help the staff grow educationally and develop the students in the same manner, his leadership will be group-centered.

If it is group-centered, leadership at the moment of action will
belong to the person who contributed toward the goal approved by
the group. If leadership is group-centered, ideas will determine its
location. If leadership is group-centered, all routes toward the objective will be explored and new creative approaches will be born,

[26] Association for Supervision and Curriculum Development, *Leadership for
Improving Instruction,* 1960 Yearbook, (Washington, D.C.: National Education
Association, 1960), p. 27.

[27] Matthew B. Miles, *Learning to Work in Groups* (New York: Teachers College, Bureau of Publications, Columbia University, 1959), p. 21.

[28] Margaret E. Bennett, "Functions and Procedures in Personnel Services," in
Personnel Services in Education, op. cit., p. 106.

[29] David H. Jenkins, "Characteristics and Functions of Leadership in Instructional Groups," in *The Dynamics of Instructional Groups, op. cit.,* p. 184.

morale will be strengthened, public relations will be improved, and an increased willingness to support education will emerge. If leadership is group-centered, a meaningful in-service education program will be unavoidable, for teachers grow as individuals when they are part of a growing group. If leadership is group-centered and if teacher learnings are transferred to classrooms, democracy will be elevated and strengthened.

CHAPTER VII

In-Service Education
and Professional Relations

All public school employees need in-service education in new understandings as each relates to one another for the strengthening of democracy and for the improvement of education. Boyd H. Bode and others claim that we inherited our method of school control from "the educational patterns of aristocratic Europe." [1] These patterns determine our human relations in school and home and in our society in general. "Control" is to most lay people a criterion of good teaching. As has been pointed out, not only have we acquired this authoritarian concept for teacher-student relationships, but we have acquired the same concept of relationship between levels of power among the professional personnel of a school system.

All people in education should re-examine their methods of relating to others. Correction of faulty practices will require effort and carefully planned in-service education programs dealing with this very human experience.

Those with foresight and an understanding of the role of the school in perpetuating democracy have urged that school practice move away from authoritarian behavior. At the very beginning of this century, John Dewey said: "The tragic weakness of the present school is that it endeavors to prepare future members of the social order in a medium in which the conditions of the social spirit are eminently wanting." [2]

This same need for teaching and living democracy in order to help the young more effectively to approach the goals of education has been urged through the years. William H. Kilpatrick claims the student must "have the vital experience of living with others in ways

---

[1] Boyd H. Bode, *Democracy As A Way of Life* (New York: The Macmillan Company, 1939), p. 64.

[2] John Dewey, *The School and Society* (Chicago: University of Chicago Press, 1900), p. 28.

that develop a loyalty to social relationships which springs from a lively concern to cooperate intelligently in the building of a better group life." [3]

Democracy, as these writers describe it, has grown out of the experiences of the race and its ideals have been perpetuated by thoughtful individuals who have sought freedom for all people.

The two major differences between democratic schools and those under autocratic control are the methods of learning and living in the school and the obligation the school has to help each student to be free to think differently from others if he so chooses. Earl J. McGrath has expressed this by saying: "Where totalitarianism demands uniformity of thought and conformity in action, democracy encourages dissent and an independent spirit." [4]

Democracy in operation insists that the group concerned must have both the freedom to establish the objectives toward which the members will work and the choice of the possible routes to be followed in working toward the goal. The school administration under these circumstances has a major responsibility in providing conditions under which work can be pursued in terms of affable working relations among the persons concerned. Unless one can relate on a mature basis to others seeking answers to the same problem, he is unable to contribute to the growth of others or to receive help from them.

William Van Til [5] has indicated that some people regard democracy in the United States as an unending experiment. This point of view, it is believed, is correct, but to perpetuate the experiment the schools need to play a larger role.

Because it is believed that teachers, principals, superintendents, and all other professional members of the school staff largely determine the climate for growth by the way they relate to each other, it has been deemed appropriate to include several reports of studies dealing with concepts of appropriate relationships in professional work. The assumption is that if a person relates freely on an inter-

---

[3] William H. Kilpatrick, *et al.*, eds., *The Educational Frontier* (New York: Appleton-Century-Crofts, 1933), p. 193.

[4] Earl James McGrath, *Education, The Wellspring of Democracy* (Tuscaloosa, Alabama: University of Alabama Press, 1951), p. 120.

[5] William Van Til, "The American Democratic Experiment," *Educational Leadership*, Vol. 17, No. 1 (October, 1959), 6–10.

personal basis, he possesses such concepts that will enable him to
act democratically in his regular school assisnment. The degree to
which educators can work on an interpersonal basis indicates their
success or lack of success in living through learning principles of
democratic behavior.

Uncertainty of Relationships in Democratic Action Among Educational Leaders

Educational leaders do not agree either on the role the school
should play in perpetuating democratic concepts or on the role they
themselves should play in terms of human relations as a model in
an administrative or a face-to-face capacity. In 1961 a series of
statements was submitted to 135 professional association leaders in
Utah [6] to determine their opinions concerning human relations as a
part of democratic procedures in school district association affairs
or in general school relationships. Each participant was given a
series of 16 statements (all expressing some aspect of human relations) with written instructions to designate one's convictions as
"True," "Probably true," "Insufficient information to have convictions," "Probably false," or "False." Although the democratic ideal
appeared to be dominant, it was not universal. The importance of
the problem lies in the fact that all of the 135 people concerned
were educational leaders. Most of them were presidents of county
or city teacher associations.

Uncertainty of democratic values may be noted by some responses. For example, 50 per cent wrote "True" or "Probably true"
to the statement: "Leaders must direct, control, motivate, and some-
times even coerce most people to get them to put forth adequate
effort toward the goals of the organization." In contrast, 41 per cent
indicated this was "Probably false" or "False."

Indicating more of this uncertainty, 27 per cent of the 135 educational leaders designated as "True" or "Probably true" the statement: "The capacity to show imagination, ingenuity, and creativity
in the solution of organizational problems is possessed by only a
very limited number of people." On the other hand, 31 per cent

---

[6] These people at the time were engaged in "training" in a leadership school.

declared the statement to be "False" and an additional 32 per cent asserted it to be "Probably false."

One more illustration indicating diverse opinions about attitudes concerned with behavior in relation to responsibility may be noted as follows: 42 per cent designated as "True" or "Probably true" the statement: "The average person prefers to be led, wishes to avoid responsibility, and wants security above all else." To this same statement 24 per cent wrote "False," and 26 per cent wrote "Probably false." These and other items of evidence clearly indicate that many educational "leaders" do not have a common opinion about democratic procedures in working with groups.

Attitudes toward Working
Relations in Provo City Schools

An opinionnaire was submitted to 242 teachers in the Provo City, Utah, schools and to 17 administrative and supervisory personnel with whom these particular teachers are associated. The statements primarily describe working relations and the development of leadership. Those interviewed were asked not to sign their own names. The respondents were asked to designate each statement as "True," "Probably true," "Insufficient information to know," "Probably false," or "False." The results indicate that opinions differ considerably on certain items, and that strong agreement exists on others. A high incidence of "True" or "False" opinions does not mean that this opinion is in keeping with research findings in social psychology or with that which may appear to be best practice. The opinionnaire likewise has the weakness common to most of this kind in that it was open to interpretation by different people.

A high per cent (70 or more) of both teachers and administrators designated as "True" or "Probably true" the following statements:

1. "The most effective leadership is that which develops as a result of the interaction of teachers' analyzing problems of common concern."
2. "Leadership potential manifests itself most conspicuously by situational insights and an eagerness to share knowledge."
3. "Teachers resist change if the administration has not helped them see the necessity for change."
4. "Evaluating the quality of teaching is the task of all professional people within a given school for that school or for all professional people within a school system."

More than 60 per cent of both groups designated as "True" or "Probably true" the statement: "Leadership may best be characterized by the status leader attempting to develop potential leadership of all members of a group interested in a problem of common interest."

A high agreement exists between the 242 teachers and the 17 administrative-supervisory personnel on some statement which over 70 per cent rated as "False" or "Probably false." Among these were the following:

1. "An evaluation of one's teaching should be made exclusively by the teacher concerned."
2. "The central school district office administrative personnel should decide the objectives of education."
3. "Group solidarity is better maintained with a strong status leader (such as a principal or school system supervisor) than in those instances wherein interest and information tend to designate the leader."

One conspicuous feature appeared repeatedly from the answers given. It is apparent that both groups (particularly the teachers) lacked a uniform opinion on certain items that clearly indicate the kind of relations that should exist if democratic principles were operative in all aspects of the school system. Almost exactly 50 per cent of the teachers wrote "True" or "Probably true" (one-third wrote "True") to the statement: "A school system is likely to have higher pupil achievement (in academic subjects) by adopting a curriculum clearly and specifically in advance than in situations where teachers weekly study curriculum problems." None of the administrative-supervisory personnel recorded this as "True."

A much higher per cent of the administrators believed the following statement to be "False" than was the case among the teachers: "Research that results from a person trained as a 'researcher' is likely to have a greater impact on the curriculum than action research emerging from that designed by the group." And, considerably more administrators than teachers believed the following statement to be "False" (no administrator wrote "True" for this statement): "When an individual clearly exhibits signs of leadership in one group situation, it is generally certain that the same person will exhibit comparable leadership roles in other situations."

Attitudes of Utah School Superintendents
and Supervisors on Work Relationships

The same opinionnaire that was used in Provo was sent to the 39 Utah city and county superintendents and to all others listed in the school directory in supervisory or related assignments. Returns were received as follows: 34 elementary school supervisors, 23 secondary school superivsors, and six persons listed as "director of curriculum." Seventy-four per cent (29 of the 39) of the superintendents and 82 per cent of the others responded to the opinionnaire. As in the case of the above-mentioned study, there were both significant differences and significant similarities. It is assumed that those in the category of "curriculum director" were too few in number to assure reliability except in such instances as their opinions may parallel others.

All groups agreed (80 per cent said "True" and 20 per cent wrote "Probably true") to the statement: "Teachers resist change if the administration has not helped them see the necessity for change." A large proportion of all groups agreed with the statement: "Evaluating the quality of teaching is the task of all professional people within a given school for that school or of all professional people within a school system for the school system."

Approximately 90 per cent of the different groups designated as "True" or "Probably true" the statement: "The most effective leadership is that which develops as a result of the interaction of teachers' analyzing problems of common concern."

There was substantial agreement among all groups to list as "False" the statements: "Any evaluation of one's teaching should be made exclusively by the teacher concerned"; and "The central school district office administrative personnel should decide the objectives of education." Other items also won a nearly universal acceptance; on some, however, there were some important differences. A substantially higher per cent of the supervisors (particularly those listed in the elementary school category) as compared to the superintendents listed as "True" the statement: "Teachers grow professionally more effectively in those situations where leadership shifts from person to person without regard to status or position."

A very noticeable difference of opinion between the superintendents and the supervisors (particularly the elementary supervisors) was expressed in the statement: "Group solidarity is better maintained with a strong status leader (such as a principal or school system supervisor) than in those instances wherein interest and information tend to designate the leader." The ratio of superintendents who considered this statement "True" was higher than 10:1.

More than two-thirds of the elementary supervisors designated as "True" the statement: "Leadership potential manifests itself most conspicuously by situational insights and an eagerness to share knowledge." Forty-one per cent of the superintendents wrote "True" to the above statement. The same approximate ratios wrote "True" to the statement: "The person playing the role of supervisor tends to create a barrier of productive action by teachers if he operates in the role of delegated authority from the central school district office."

"Opinions" in Relation to Democracy in Teaching

Some observations of the above statements of professional people appear to be important if we assume democratic behavior in the schools is needed as a means of in-service education and as a model for students. It should be repeated that an instrument such as that used has certain weaknesses. The probability exists that any statements such as these may be understood or interpreted differently by different respondents. The possibility also exists, in spite of the fact that the answers were unsigned, that the professional person attempted to write the "correct" answer rather than indicating the way he felt or what characterized his behavior in relating to others.

It may be noted that almost all administrative and supervisory personnel possess at least a master's degree. Some of this group have a doctorate and most have taken graduate work beyond the master's degree. All of the Provo teachers have a minimum of a bachelor's degree and slightly more than 40 per cent have a master's degree. Some have accumulated considerable graduate credit.

The most apparent characteristic of all groups (as groups) is that there are relatively wide differences of opinion about the role of the professional person in relation to democratic behavior. An examination of individual responses indicates a high degree of consistency. That is, if the respondent believed the administrator as a status person possessed all the qualities of leadership and control, he believed it to be true in all situations. On the other hand, those who expressed opinions that were strongly democratic in their relations with others maintained them under all relational situations.

Opinions concerned with democratic relationships between teachers and administrative personnel in Provo are more alike than are the opinions of administrators and supervisors throughout the state as a whole. This is true in spite of the differences mentioned above.

The proportion of elementary supervisors in the state believing in democratic behavior is the highest of any of the groups.

The only information requested of respondents was the "number of years of professional education experience."

The people who had served in excess of five years expressed a greater preference for democratic behavior than did those with less than five years. Forty-two of the Provo teachers were in their first year of teaching, and these possessed convictions that were more autocratic than those of any other group. This may indicate a feeling of insecurity and a need for relying on a status person for help, or it may mean that they thought this was the "correct" answer. Certainly, it does imply that an in-service education program is needed for them before their autocratic behavior becomes habitual in the classroom.

One may conclude from an examination of the 322 opinionnaires that important differences appear in regard to the kinds of relationships that should exist in a given school or a school system. A relatively large proportion have an image of the status person as one who should exhibit democratic behavior, but many do not possess such an image, and some see such a person in an anti-democratic role.

A School Studies Teacher-Student Relations

The 18 teachers in one elementary school decided to study thei. teacher-student relations and prepared their own method of study as a part of an in-service education program.

The study proceeded as follows: All teachers spent approximately a month in reviewing the literature concerned with teaching methods, teacher-child relations, motivation, and other items related to learning and teaching. The faculty met weekly for a minimum of an hour, made reports, exchanged experiences, and did additional planning and evaluating. At the end of the first month, when the reading-discussion-study was completed, each teacher made a tape recording of his own verbal interaction with the students for approximately twenty to thirty minutes. The time was of sufficient length to make a reproduction of various kinds of teacher-student reacting.

The teacher used a neck microphone as he moved from place to place within the classroom. Three other upright microphones were strategically placed in the room. Each teacher was given instruction on the method of using the equipment and demonstrated such an ability as part of the training but was alone with the students when the tapes were recorded. A few trial runs were made for the purpose of eliminating the novelty of the recording equipment to the students. With the use of this recording apparatus, the teacher periodically made a series of tapes for his personal study.

Teachers then played back the records for their own analysis. The original plan was to limit the playback to the teacher concerned for his personal use. But it was also in the plan for teachers to make as many records as they wanted if they had a goal toward which they were working. The goal soon became one of the teacher doing much less talking and finding ways by which the student or students would respond more. The plan of keeping the record personal soon was replaced by the plan of having fellow teachers analyze the records. Teachers seemed particularly delighted to note the decreasing ratio of time they talked and the decreasing number of "directives" or "controls" they made when they did talk.

Four conclusions were made leading toward a successful in-service education program that may readily be used by other teacher groups. First, a careful (though brief) study of current literature helps to build some important concepts of successful teaching indicating good teacher-student relations; second, faculty discussions are productive in placing a focus at the point of needed change; third, accurate records can be made cheaply and used by teachers for analyzing their own and student behavior; and fourth, teachers can observe their own rate of growth toward the goal they have established.

During the process of making these tape recordings some teachers invited their colleagues into the classroom to record both teacher and student nonverbal behavior thought to have an effect on the teaching-learning process. Needless to say, this added to the value of the record for teacher analysis and effort to improve.

It was agreed that each teacher would write a brief statement of one or two impressions. Almost universally, the following declaration was made: "I did too much directing of children during the first recordings but by purposeful effort was able to change and get substantially more student participation indicating added learning."

The above descriptions indicate that there is evidence that teachers can make changes toward a more democratic approach by persistent effort. It is highly possible that teachers' greatest need in in-service education is in experiencing interaction with other teachers and with students if democracy is to be learned and lived by those who spend their days in school.

CHAPTER VIII

The Use of a Code as a
Means of In-Service Education

Many books and articles have been written in which attempts have been made to describe the best methods of teaching. It has been assumed generally that if the neophyte can perceive a model of excellent teaching he will attempt to imitate this model in an effort toward developing teaching effectiveness. It is recognized, however, that teaching involves very complex behavior and that excellent teaching of a given kind or in a given situation may not be appropriate under differing circumstances.

The public within the past dozen years has developed increased interest in so-called quality teaching, and the schools everywhere are under pressure to improve teaching. Needless to say, the concepts of good teaching held by the public and, probably to a lesser degree, by the teachers themselves vary greatly. Understanding teachers express concern because much of the pressure coming from the public would not only retard progress but would require teachers to return to earlier methods.

Among the suggestions commonly made by the public is that of "merit" salary increases for what is deemed to be superior teaching in contrast to that which is thought to be mediocre. It is assumed that salary differences will motivate the so-called poorer teacher to improve. It was not uncommon twenty-five or more years ago for school systems to use rating instruments as a basis for salary differentials. A more careful study of such scales, coupled with accumulating information of the teaching-learning process, convinced school personnel that these rating plans were inadequate. The principal difficulties were three: (1) the person using the rating scale necessarily made a subjective rating; (2) the one doing the rating had no known criteria or standards that were usable in making the evaluation; and (3) this method of rating tended to decrease morale and raised barriers of ill-will which prevented good communications among the professional staff.

Initiating the Provo, Utah,
Plan of Merit Study

The widespread public belief in a need for teacher rating for meritorious teaching reached the Utah legislature, which created a state committee of lay and school people and gave this committee the responsibility of establishing an investigation of possible methods of identifying "meritorious" teaching. Three school districts were selected as experimental districts. One of these was Provo City School District, the only one that conducted the study during the six years that the study was financed by the state.

A contractual agreement was made between the Provo Board of Education and the State of Utah to perpetuate the study during the first two-year period. This was done at the request (by private vote) of a substantial majority of the teachers in the school district. The school district was given complete freedom to develop the program in any way it might choose. Its only legal obligation was to pursue the study during the time the state provided the money. The state did employ a director, but the school system had complete control of the research program. The legislature renewed its financial obligation periodically, making funds available for six years. The committee worked in the offices of the board of education and was under the general supervision of the superintendent of schools. During the six-year study the committee had a full-time director and some five or six other people who worked full- or part-time. Consultants from different universities were also employed. Many other professional personnel contributed their time—some only a few hours in which they heard progress reports, asked questions deemed to be of significance, or made recommendations. This group included most of the psychologists and many members of the colleges of education from all of the higher institutions in Utah. Moreover, the Provo administrative-supervisory personnel spent considerable time in evaluating proposed possible approaches and in making recommendations or developing issues that needed clarification.

Attempts to Define and Describe
Quality Teaching

A major task during all six years was to find an objective way to define or describe the qualitative aspects of teaching. Early in the study it became apparent that any definition or description of teaching must have the qualities of validity and reliability. In order to analyze teaching—i.e., to perceive what one does when he teaches and to understand differences in teaching—it was decided to get written specimens of the teaching-learning process. In order to obtain a cross section of teaching it became necessary to gather samples or specimens from many teachers in different situations. Different methods of securing these samples were tried. At first, teachers would teach for twenty or thirty minutes and then attempt to write as accurately as possible what had been said (and to describe other forms of behavior) by teacher and students during that time. This method lacked reliability. An improvement on this method was to have a trained stenographer record everything that was said and by whom, while a trained observer made notes of nonverbal behavior at the same time. Another method involved photographing or using sensitive recording machines by making a tape record of that which each person said during a given time (usually about thirty minutes), while a trained observer made notes of nonverbal behavior. At least three records were made of different situations for all teacher records that were used.

Six hundred forty-eight elementary school teacher records and 270 secondary school teacher records from Provo City Schools and over 50 selected teachers elsewhere in Utah and in other states were used for study analysis and use.

To obtain additional insight into teaching, partial records were made of "assumed" excellent teaching and "assumed" mediocre teaching in several (usually large) city systems in different states of the nation. (These teachers were selected by administrative-supervisory personnel acquainted with the teachers' teaching.) This large number of different records was examined, classified, and codified. It could then be stated with a high degree of accuracy that "this is what teachers and children do as the teaching-learning process takes place."

The Development of a Code

These teaching records were examined and analyzed to make a code. Each one of the subdivisions of the code was given a name or a descriptive term. These terms were descriptive of the functions performed (or the behavior) by the teacher while teaching. The committee became convinced from an examination of all records that teacher functions fall in six major categories:

1. Functions that control;
2. Functions that facilitate;
3. Functions that develop content by response;
4. Functions that serve as personal response;
5. Functions of positive affectivity;
6. Functions of negative affectivity.

Under each of these major functions were "secondary functions" and "subfunctions of the secondary functions." For example, under "Functions that control" are five subfunctions all indicating a function of control. One of these subfunctions is listed in the code as "Regulate." However, the teacher "regulates" in several different ways, it was noted from the records. Consequently, it was necessary to categorize or list in more detail the subfunctions. These listings include "Open" (i.e., open regulating), "Closed," "Routine," and others.

Examples of coding a record under the general category of "Functions of negative affectivity" are such as "Admonish," "Reprimand," "Accusative," and "Verbal futuristic." Needless to say, the terminology may not be understandable to the reader who has not analyzed the code, but the terms do have meaning when one learns to use the code with a high degree of accuracy. Some other terminology may be equally meaningful, and changes may be made with more use of the code. It is important to categorize the teaching records by understanding the various kinds of teacher-student behavior. Moreover, it is important that the teacher use a given record and place each teaching incident or item of behavior in a given category so that after a lapse of time he can take the same record and accurately categorize it as was done in the earlier situation. It is likewise important that two or more trained professional personnel categorize a given record in identical or nearly identical fashion.

Determining Reliability and Validity

A special effort was made to develop an instrument, later called the Provo Code, that would have the qualities of objectivity, reliability, and validity. As inferred above, the code would have no value unless two or more professional educators could be trained to use it to analyze a teaching record and classify the items of teaching in a similar manner. This was done as part of the study. It is not claimed that no differences in codification will appear when two trained persons codify a record. It is claimed that a high degree of accuracy in similarity of categorizing can be expected. On the occasional differences that may appear, the coders attempted to arrive at a consensus as to the code item most likely to be descriptive of the given item of behavior.

In order to determine more accurately the validity and reliability of the code it appeared necessary to determine the degree of accuracy that may be displayed by other professional educators who had not helped to devise the code. Two elementary school principals were selected for this purpose. Their training involved an understanding and memorization (at least, a partial memorization) of the terminology of the code as descriptive terms of the incidents of teaching-learning behavior in the records. Measures of the principals' learning were made from time to time. Progress was slow at first but improved rapidly as memorizations and insights were established. Different methods of determining the accuracy and rate of improvement were established by comparing the number of right and wrong codifications with those who had earlier become proficient in the codification process and who had helped make the code. The principals were paired for comparison with those deemed experts, and then "crossed," each working with an expert for a consensus on the codification of the several items of behavior. The principals made more rapid progress when working with an expert than when paired together, and more progress when paired together than when working alone.

It is believed that evidence was sufficient to justify a conviction that professional educators can be trained to use the code with a high degree of accuracy for the purpose of codifying a record of teaching and learning.

It may be noted that certain items of teaching were coded with a higher degree of accuracy than were other items. This probably suggests that with prolonged research certain terminology of the code (as a descriptive term) may be changed or other refinements made. On the other hand, it was learned that not all teaching behavior is easy to describe or define.

The Code and Role-Playing

In order further to analyze the reliability and validity of the code and to determine whether or not the code could be used to help teachers improve the quality of teaching, two of the faculties of the smaller elementary schools in Provo agreed to spend periodic study evenings with the merit study directors and to attempt to learn the code and find its applications in their effort to improve teaching. This program was conducted during one school year. It was agreed after examining some teaching records and developing a partial understanding of the code to do some role-playing of teaching for the purpose of determining whether the code could be used to differentiate between good and mediocre teaching.

The role-playing consisting of a series of acts agreed to by all participants and assumed to be comparable to the incidents that may daily occur in the classroom. Two volunteer teachers would do the role-playing as teachers: one playing what was assumed to be a teaching incident of high quality, and the other playing an incident of mediocre teaching. The remaining teachers acted as students to make the situation as nearly typical as possible under the circumstances. After the role-playing, the teachers analyzed the two different roles and suggested possible alterations that may improve the better teaching incidents and likewise made suggestions that would tend to make the less effective role of a poorer quality. Transcribed records were made of all role-playing, with copies provided to each participating teacher so that he might study them and make such modifications thought desirable in actual teaching during the following days.

Participating teachers became convinced that the code can be used as a very effective method of in-service training. It provides a means of firsthand observation of good and poor teaching, provides frank discussion of the qualities of teaching incidents, enables the teacher to examine the record critically with the use of the code, and motivates the teacher in an attempt to improve his own teaching in actual situations.

In the analysis of the "good" as compared to the "poor" teaching, it was found that the functions of control and negative affectivity occurred with substantially more frequency in the "poor" teaching than in the "good" teaching. In contrast, teacher behavior that was classified as positive affectivity and other code classifications indicating teacher-student relations that were conducive to facilitating the ongoing program by responding to personal student needs were much more common in "good" teaching.

Experts' Evaluation of Teacher Records

In an attempt to increase the probability that the code may be used as a helpful instrument in differentiating quality in teaching, it was decided to select ten specimen teaching records and to have them judged as to quality by a panel of seven experts. These teaching records were obtained from teachers in two different states on a basis of qualitative differences, and it was assumed they would vary in quality from very good to poor, although they were all records taken from actual classroom situations.

The panel of experts was selected on the basis of nominations by known scholars. Letters were sent to fifty professional people in different parts of the nation, all of whom had nationwide reputations in the field of teaching and learning, requesting them to nominate "from three to five" persons they believed to be most capable to serve on such a panel. The seven selected were those most frequently nominated. To each of these were sent the ten specimen teaching records. The panel was asked to place them in order of rank from "best" to "poorest" and to make any notation thought to be appropriate designating how the best specimen might further be improved or how the poorest one might be made poorer without greatly altering the apparent intent of the teacher.

There was a high degree of agreement in the ranking of the records. All seven panel members, each working alone, designated the same record as the poorest. All but two selected the same record as "next to poorest." One of the panel gave this next to poorest record a rank of "8" and one gave it a rank of "7."

There was high agreement in the rankings of the "best" two or three records but not to the same degree as was the case of the "poorest." In fact, each one of the panel members tended to rank the records in close agreement with all other members of the panel.

The written comments that were submitted were those that would have given the students more freedom of expression or positive affectivity in the records deemed best, and in contrast would have used more directives and controls or negative affectivity in the poorest records.

Use of the Code to Improve Teaching

The basic concern of the Provo committee during the six-year study was that of identifying differences in teacher-pupil relations that characterize differences in the quality of teaching. After the code was developed, refined, and after the committee had used it for about four years in analyzing teacher records, it was planned to use it by the two faculties mentioned above in order to find an answer to the question: Can teachers learn the code sufficiently well that it may serve as a guide to improve teaching?

The teachers from these two schools were given some released time to meet with the committee for study purposes. The meetings (held once or twice a week) were informal and characterized by interest and high morale.

It was agreed that each participating teacher would have a record made of his own (typical) teaching in the autumn and another record of his teaching in the spring, thereby allowing approximately a six-month interval for study purposes. The code was used to categorize the two records to determine changes (and progress, if any) in teacher behavior during the interval. The most conspicuous differences between the two records (in the main, these differences occurred with all participating teachers) for each teacher was the decrease from autumn to spring in the number and per cent of major functions that were categorized as controlling and the increase in development of content and positive affectivity.[1] Important changes were also made in secondary functions and in subfunctions, all indicating trends in the direction of theoretical progress.

All teachers did not make the same amount of change but as a group did report that their study of the code and meeting together to discuss its use was a means of "helping them in the improvement of their own teaching." [2]

It appears certain from the reports of these teachers' experiences that three statements may be made:

1. Teachers' behavior tends to become "habitual." The teacher learns what she does as she relates to and controls students.
2. In order to change "habits" in teaching it requires concentrated and continuous effort working toward an understood goal.
3. The code as developed in Provo can be learned and interpreted in such a way that it may serve as a guide in the improvement of teaching.

It is used to break down or analyze the teaching-learning incidents and to classify or codify them by their diverse functions. These functions are assumed to be the effect of the teacher behavior on the pupil. The major functions are those that (1) control, (2) facilitate, (3) develop content by response, (4) serve as personal response, (5) induce positive affectivity, and (6) induce negative affectivity.

Subsidiary to the major functions are secondary functions. These secondary functions segregate aspects of the major functions, refine the larger items of behavior, and name the various ways in which the major functions occur.

Subfunctions, delineate an even finer phase of the process and describe how a given secondary function is used. Only a limited

---

[1] Gretta P. Romney and Research Staff, *Patterns of Effective Teaching,* Second Progress Report (June, 1961), 59.
[2] *Ibid.,* p. 89.

TABLE 1
OUTLINE OF THE PROVO CODE FOR THE ANALYSIS OF TEACHING

FUNCTIONS THAT CONTROL	FUNCTIONS THAT FACILITATE	FUNCTIONS THAT DEVELOP CONTENT BY RESPONSE	FUNCTIONS THAT SERVE AS PERSONAL RESPONSE	FUNCTIONS OF POSITIVE AFFECTIVITY	FUNCTIONS OF NEGATIVE AFFECTIVITY
Structure open closed sequential oriented intervening public criteria	*Checking* information routine involvement	*Resource* routine student oriented	*Meets Request* positive negative makes arrangements	*Support* stereotype specific	*Admonish*
Regulate open closed global routine neutral sequential self public criteria	*Demonstrate*	*Stimulate*	*Clarify problem*	*Solicitous*	*Reprimand*
Inform	*Clarify Procedure*	*Structure turn-back*	*Interprets* situation feelings teacher action	*Encourage*	*Accusative*
Standard Set recall teacher edict group developed universal		*Clarify* content experience generalize summarize		*Does For Personal*	
Judge teacher directed punishing turned back moralize		*Evaluate* positive negative public criteria		*Teacher Estimate of Need*	*Verbal Futuristic*

October, 1959

number of definitions and examples may be used to explain the process of coding.

Structuring is done by the teacher when he indicates the situation to which students are expected to respond. For example, he states: "Get your history books and read the first paragraph on page 200." Structuring thus tends to give direction to which the student will respond. If it is "structure open," it does not prescribe an exact response. On the other hand, if it is "structure closed" it limits the nature of the response. If it is "structure sequential" it describes more than one response, the second and/or third depending on the previous response.

Functions of positive affectivity affect the behavior of the child positively and tend to establish feelings of relating to the teacher or the situation in a pleasant manner. The teacher gives support in positive affectivity by concurring or expressing approval of the student's response. The incident is coded as "support solicitous" when a teacher says: "Fred, your writing is improving. Can you continue this trend?"

It is negative affectivity—admonishing—when a teacher says, "If you don't stand away from this bandsaw, you will lose a finger."

Limitations and Values of the Code

It is believed that the code does have significant value as a means of improving one's teaching. It can be understood sufficiently well so that teachers can build their own perception or image of good teaching. Although it can be used to distinguish good from poor teaching, claim is not made that it can be used to make extremely fine differences in small items of teaching. It is believed that it or some comparable instrument may be used as an excellent device for in-service education of teachers. It is believed that it can be used by teachers who are teaching any age or grade group.

The code needs additional refinement with perhaps several more years of research. In its present form it is complex to the point of being cumbersome unless the one who uses it can interpret it and can memorize much of its content. It is readily noted by one who examines the code that it is used primarily to examine the verbal responses of teachers and students, making it desirable to have an assistant professional person who records nonverbal behavior of the teacher and the students and makes the notation at the correct place in the record. Under these circumstances, people with proper training can make effective use of categorizing teacher records.

A general statement may be made indicating that this code or some comparable instrument can be a device that describes effective and ineffective teaching behavior. In-service education programs may develop such instruments. Under such conditions the instrument should be written—i.e., descriptive of successful teaching behavior in order that teachers may learn preferred behavior. Constant effort should then be maintained to develop an image of excellent teaching and to attempt to imitate the excellence of the image. The image, however, must not be one image that may invite uniformity in teaching but an over-all pattern of interaction with children that invites individual growth of teachers and children.

Teacher Evaluations and In-Service Education

Industry has made attempts to make differences in wage scales based upon efficiency or production. Some claim these are successful, and others believe this is not so. The real fact is that teaching is different from working on a production line where articles or produce in packages can be counted and where any deviation from the standard article is a sign of a defect. Education is both a process and, in a sense, an end. Education serves to make people alike and to make them different. Consequently, any evaluation or rating program intended to improve the quality of teaching will be confronted with problems which are not present in the production of material goods.

Teaching changes—it is never the same from moment to moment. It is for this reason that a permanent standard or criterion cannot be established.

Douglass, Bent, and Boardman, among scores of others, have pointed out the problems involved in determining or predicting teacher ability due to a lack of valid criteria. They specifically state: "The evaluation of teaching efficiency must still depend largely upon subjective judgment, the development of objective techniques of measurement [are] lying largely in the future." [3]

Evidence appears to be abundant that teacher ratings as yet developed do not improve the quality of teaching. Rating instruments, as such, do little to serve in effective in-service education programs.

---

[3] Harl R. Douglass, Rudyard K. Bent, and Charles W. Boardman, *Democratic Supervision in Secondary Schools,* 2nd ed. (Cambridge, Mass.: The Riverside Press, 1961), p. 125.

Bibliography

Association for Supervision and Curriculum Development, Part II, *Group Planning in Education*. Washington, D.C.: National Education Association, 1945. Pp. 130–53.

———, *Action for Curriculum Improvement*. Washington, D.C.: National Education Association, 1951. Pp. 1–244.

———, *Balance in the Curriculum*. Washington, D.C.: National Education Association, 1961. Pp. 1–194.

———, *Continuing Growth for the Teacher. (Educational Leadership.)* Washington. D.C.: National Education Association, November, 1962.

———, *Leadership for Improving Instruction*. Washington, D.C.: National Education Association, 1960. Pp. 1–191.

———, *Perceiving, Behaving, Becoming*. Washington, D.C.: National Education Association, 1962. Pp. 1–253.

American Association of School Administrators, *The Superintendent As Instructional Leader,* Thirty-Fifth Yearbook, 1957. Pp. 1–484.

Bode, Boyd H., *Democracy As A Way of Life*. New York: The Macmillan Company, 1939. Pp. 1–113.

Burton, William H. and Leo J. Bruechner, *Supervision: A Social Process,* 2nd ed. New York: Appleton-Century-Crofts, Inc., 1955.

Department of Elementary School Principals, National Education Association, *In-Service Growth of School Personnel,* Twenty-First Yearbook. Washington, D.C.: National Education Association, 1942. Pp. 1–347.

Douglass, Harl R., Rudyard K. Bent, and Charles W. Boardman, *Democratic Supervision in Secondary Schools,* 2nd ed. Boston: Houghton Mifflin Company, 1961. Chaps. 3, 4, 5, 10.

Gordon, Thomas, *Group-Centered Leadership*. Boston: Houghton Mifflin Company, 1955. Pp. 1–366.

Gwynn, J. Minor, *Theory and Practice of Supervision*. New York: Dodd, Mead & Co., 1961. Pp. 1–449.

Hicks, Hanne J., *Educational Supervision in Principle and Practice*. New York: The Ronald Press Company, 1960. Pp. 1–425.

Hildreth, Gertrude H., "Evaluation of a Workshop in Education," *Teachers College Record,* Vol. 46, No. 5. (February, 1945), 310–19.

Kelley, Earl C., *The Workshop Way of Learning*. New York: Harper & Row, Publishers, 1951. Pp. 1–163.

Lane, Howard and Mary Beauchamp, *Human Relations in Teaching.* Englewood Cliffs, N.J.: Prentice-Hall, Inc., 1955. Pp. 1–346.

Maccoby, Eleanor E., Theodore M. Newcomb, and Eugene L. Hartley, eds., *Readings in Social Psychology,* 3rd ed. New York: Holt, Rinehart & Winston, Inc., 1958. Chaps. 11, 12, 13.

Miles, Matthew B., *Learning to Work in Groups.* New York: Teachers College, Bureau of Publications, Columbia University, 1959. Pp. 1–285.

Miller, George and Research Staff, "Progress Report of Merit Study of Provo City Schools." Provo, Utah: Office of Board of Education. Pp. 1–224. Unpublished.

Mitchell, James R., "The Workshop As An In-Service Education Procedure," *North Central Association Quarterly,* Vol. 28 (1953–54), 421–57.

Moffitt, John C., "Administration of In-Service Teacher Education," *Educational Administration,* Vol. 37 (October, 1951), 355–61.

National Commission on Teacher Education, National Education Association, "Policies Relating to In-Service Growth of Teachers," *Journal of Teacher Education,* Vol. III (June, 1952), 1–114.

National Society for the Study of Education, *Citizen Cooperation for Better Schools,* Nelson B. Henry, ed., Vol. 53, Part I. Chicago: University of Chicago Press, 1954. Pp. 1–304.

————, *In-Service Education,* Vol. 56, Part II. Chicago: University of Chicago Press, 1957. Pp. 1–367.

————, *Individualizing Instruction,* Vol. 61, Part I. Chicago: University of Chicago Press, 1962. Pp. 1–337.

————, *Personnel Services in Education,* Vol. 58, Part II. Chicago: University of Chicago Press, 1959. Pp. 1–303.

————, *The Dynamics of Instructional Groups,* Vol. 59, Part II. Chicago: University of Chicago Press, 1960. Pp. 1–286.

Parker, J. Cecil and William P. Golden, Jr., "In-Service Education of Elementary- and Secondary-School Teachers," *Review of Educational Research,* Vol. 22 (June, 1952), 193–200.

Romney, Gretta P. and Research Staff, "Patterns of Effective Teaching." Second Progress Report of Merit Study, Provo City Schools. Provo, Utah: Office of Board of Education, June 1961. Pp. 1–52. Unpublished.

Rummel, J. Francis, *An Introduction to Research Procedures in Education.* New York: Harper & Row, Publishers, 1958. Pp. 1–413.

Sharp, George, *Curriculum Development As Re-education of the Teachers.* New York: Teachers College, Bureau of Publications, Columbia University, 1951. Pp. 1–132.

Spears, Harold, *Curriculum Planning Through In-Service Programs.* Englewood Cliffs, N.J.: Prentice-Hall, Inc., 1957. Pp. 1–350.

Swearingen, Mildred E., *Supervision of Instruction: Foundations and Dimensions.* Boston: Allyn and Bacon, Inc., 1962. Pp. 1–307.

Thelen, Herbert A., *Dynamics of Groups at Work.* Chicago: University of Chicago Press, 1954. Pp. 1–379.

Wood, Hugh B., "In-Service Education of Teachers, An Evaluation," *Journal of Teacher Education*, Vol. 2 (December, 1951), 243–47.

Yauch, Wilbur A., *Improving Human Relations in School Administration.* New York: Harper & Row, Publishers, 1940. Pp. 1–299.

Index

Index

111